Just for you!

TO:

I bought this book **just for you**. I hope you like it too! Remember, hot gets cold and fresh gets stale but my thoughts of you will always prevail.

FROM:

The following trademarks appear throughout this cookbook: Hollandaise Sauce, Van de Kamp, Wondra Flour, Crisco, Nestles Chocolate, Morrell Lard, Jello, Best Yet, Cedar Hill, Rotel, LaChoy, Cool Whip, Ashley, Pet Milk, Longhorn Cheese, Tyson Chicken, Mid-American Monterey Jack, Aunt Harriet's, Braum's Butter, Pam, Eagle Condensed Milk, Carton Whipped Cream, Old El Paso Taco Sauce, Rose Brand, Sharp, Padre Jalapeno, Aquafarms Catfish, Griffin, Dox-Chili, Paul Newman Salad Dressing, Dijon Mustard, Lawry's Seasoned Salt, Worcestershire Sauce, Toll House, Doritos, 7 UP, J-M Farms, Shawnee Mills, Orbit, Farm Fresh, Maria-Rae's Salsa, Kitchen Bouquet, Bake-rite, Cedar Hill.

Although the author and publisher have exhaustively researched all the sources to ensure the accuracy and completeness of the information contained in this cookbook, we assume no responsibility for errors, inaccuracies, omissions or any other inconsistency herein. Any slights against people or organizations are unintentional.

Copyright © 1995   Joe Fiorentino

The Famous People Cookbook, What's Cookin' in the U.S.A.
All rights reserved. No part of this book may be reproduced in any form or by any means, electronic or mechanical including photocopying, recording or by any information storage and retrieval systems without permission in writing from the publisher, except by any reviewer, who may quote brief passages or recipes in a review. Published by
Bright Ideas in Marketing Publications, P.O. Box 494 Broomall, Pa. 19008

The Library of Congress Cataloging in Publication Data

LCCN 95-94354

ISBN 0-9646661-0-3

Attention Corporations and professional Organizations: Quantity discounts are available on bulk purchases of this book for fund raising or gift giving. Special books, booklets, or book excerpts can also be created to fit your specific needs. For information contact: **Bright Ideas in Marketing Publications P.O. Box 494 Broomall, Pa. 19008**
To order small quantities of this book, use the order form on page 160.

Printed in the United States of America.

CONTENTS

History Making

APPETIZERS
BEVERAGES
PAGE 9

BREAD
SANDWICHES
PAGE 15

CAKES
COOKIES
PAGE 25

MEAT
PAGE 51

PASTA
PAGE 65

PIES/PASTRY
PAGE 69

POULTRY
PAGE 75

RICE/EGGS
PAGE 95

SALAD
PAGE 105

SAUCE/DIPS
PAGE 116

SEAFOOD
PAGE 119

SOUP
PAGE 133

VEGETABLES
PAGE 139

TERMS
PAGE 50

WE WANT YOU
PAGE 132

NEW FOOD
LABEL
PAGE 102-103

INDEX
PAGE 152-157

ORGANIZER
PAGES 143-151

RECIPES

PREFACE

Do you believe in magic? I truly believe that something magical happens around food. The demographics involved are incredible. Food touches or should I say is touched, by people of all ages, cultures, races and socioeconomic backgrounds around the world. While there is undeniably a physiological need for food to nourish the body, good food nurtures the spirit as well.

There are also some very real social and cultural aspects of food. It invokes exchange. Whether it is at a business luncheon or at the family dinner table, many important decisions and resolutions magically come to fruition. Over a delicious, or in some unfortunate case, a not so delicious meal. With today's busy and changing lifestyles, the gathering around the table to share a meal is probably one venue that still encourages family unity and communication. It was at one such family dinner that I decided to compile this unique and resourceful cookbook.

I did not realize at the time, that working in the record business was a major component in my deciding to compile this cookbook. Over the twenty years there were two questions that kept popping up from the artists that I promoted. The questions started when I became the promotion manager for Universal Distributors'. In the five years there I learned a great deal about promotion and the record business. Universal is a great company to work for and a tough company to leave, but the offer from Warner Bros. Records was just too good to turn down. With the many artists that Warner Bros. has, the ever present two questions, became doubled. After five years they offered me the East coast regional marketing director position for Warner Bros. Records, Atlantic Records and Elektra Records. (WEA Distributing. - a Warner Communication Inc. company). My duties were to coordinate the marketing, promotion and sales for these three companies, covering the East coast. After six years in this position the two questions were still ever present. Now they were tripled.

Working in the record business in a major market, with major companies, promoting and marketing talented artists and their product, was rewarding. Each day offered new challenges and experiences, many that could not be duplicated in any other business. Major markets generate an unremitting flow of artists that are on a concert tour, or come in to the market to help promote their record. I can tell you first hand the flow of artists was unnerving.

By now you must be wondering what the two questions were that kept popping up over the twenty years in the record business. One was, What is happening with my record? Referring to sales, promotion and radio play, and the other question was the one that prompted me to compile this cookbook, WHERE ARE WE HAVING DINNER? The questions were not always in that order but the day was over and we went to have dinner. Table talk was a mixture of exchanging record business stories, information on their product and the variety of foods they enjoyed while touring the United States. In the back of my mind I knew someday, time permitting, I would compile a selection of great territorial and regional recipe favorites from across the U.S.A...

In designing this cookbook, major consideration was given to assure that every aspect was covered, offering a cookbook that will provide many basic cooking needs. Serving the novice and the experienced cook, intended not only for those who know their way around the kitchen, but also for those who are trying to find the right path.

On the pages of "The Famous People Cookbook, What's Cookin' in the U.S.A." You will find interesting proverbs that pertain to food, splendid recipes from appetizers to mouth-watering desserts, cooking and restaurant terms that may not be used every day defined and explained in easy-to-understand language, superb recipes that will allow you to reproduce firsthand in your own home the culinary preferences of many famed personalities. Even the Vice President of the United States Al Gore and Tipper Gore divulge their family's favorite roasted chicken recipe.

You can take a taste tour of America without leaving your kitchen. There are many prize winning recipes and regional favorites, including family specialities that until now handed down from generation to generation and sampled by only a lucky few. Many are indigenous to a specific region of the United States and reflect the local flavors of those areas.

Holiday Menus provided are to help ease the burden of entertaining whether it is a grand Christmas Gala or an informal summer barbecue. Suggested combinations of food that complement each other and are suitable for the specific occasion, whatever the season might be.

For beginners or very busy cooks there are easy and fun to make recipes, guaranteed to please all palates while assuring successful results with the easy-to-follow uncomplicated directions.

A practical section is the **Recipe Organizer.** We all know the frustration of trying to find that certain recipe we saw in another cookbook or magazine somewhere. The one we clipped and stashed for safekeeping only to find we hid it too well. The RECIPE ORGANIZER allows you to keep all your recipes together in one cookbook, by simply entering them onto the formatted, ready to be filled pages. Searching for that must-have, but cannot find misplaced recipe is now over!

Another useful chapter is **HOW TO READ THE NEW FOOD LABEL/ USING THE NEW FOOD LABEL TO CHOOSE HEALTHIER FOODS.** If you have not read a food label lately, you do not know what you are missing. The Federal Government has revamped the food label in a major way. Resulting in a label that is up-to-date with today's health concerns and a label that you can understand and count on to help in preparing healthy meals and snacks.

Included in the Famous People Cookbook are: Over 125 recipes, many prize winning and regional favorites, an invitation to be in the next cookbook, Gift card enclosure, free bookmarks, many heart-smart and healthy minded recipes, how to adapt Granny's recipes to healthier eating, how to cook a perfect turkey, how to carve a turkey, how to open steamed crabs, (what part you can eat) and safe food handling facts.

I hope you enjoy this cookbook and the many meals produced from its pages. Whether it is for yourself, somebody on your gift list who deserves that something special, or the bride-to-be. Or that someone that is moving into a new home, this cookbook will be the perfect addition to any kitchen.

I also would like to invite all of you who are reading this to send me your own special recipe. You can be part of our next cookbook, "We the People of the U.S.A. Cookbook." Featuring a compilation of family favorites from folks all over the U.S.A. Ask your friends and relatives to send along their favorite recipes too. The recipes cannot be returned and will become the property of the Publisher Bright Ideas in Marketing Publications. P.O. Box 494 Broomall, Pa. 19008.

Special thanks go to the many people that contributed their help and guidance. Thanks too: The staff at my local library for all their assistance. If you have not visited a library lately... GO! It's a great place with excellent selections and great service from knowledgeable, professional people. The Department of Health and Human Services, Food and Drug Administration, Food Safety and Inspection Service, The American Heart Association, U.S. Department of Agriculture, Oklahoma Dept. of Agriculture, Barbara J D'Alonzo, Marianne B Zajdel, Holiday Menu contributors' Vicki Guiteras Giunta, is Executive Producer of Stages of Imagination, Inc. and a very busy freelance actress, Cathy McGraw, mother of three beautiful children and my daughter, Gary E. Hendler, the President of Suburban Real Estate Rental and Sales, Joe Fiorentino Jr., a Penn State graduate, super football fan, and my son, Gloria F Moppert, my sister who after raising four children, set out to become a successful entrepreneur in Real Estate and retail business.

Assembling this cookbook has been fun, and I enjoyed creating it. The style is easy and casual though the contributors are people of stature. They are America's leaders confronted every day with a tremendous obligation and responsibility to govern this great country. They are the History makers of not only America... but the entire world. Through their recipes and comments, the cookbook has allowed me to present the family side of these outstanding people. Willing to take the time from their very busy schedule to share their favorite recipes for you to enjoy. Without these **HISTORY MAKERS** this cookbook would have been history. I appreciate their generosity and thank them again. Here they are and the State they represent:
Al Gore Vice President of the United States of America.
Daniel K Akaka U.S. Senator ....HAWAII
Bill P Baker Congressman .... CALIFORINA
Christopher S Bond U.S. Senator ....MISSOURI
Carol Moseley Braun U.S. Senator ....ILLINOIS
John B Breaux U.S. Senator ....LOUISIANA
Hank Brown U.S. Senator ....COLORADO
Conrad Burns U.S. Senator .... MONTANA
Carroll A Campbell Jr. Governor of.......... SOUTH CAROLINA.
James E Clyburn Congressman .... SOUTH CAROLINA
Dan Coats U.S. Senator ....INDIANA
Howard Coble Congressman ....NORTH CAROLINA
William S Cohen U.S. Senator ....MAINE
Paul Coverdell U.S. Senator ....GEORGIA
Larry E Craig U.S. Senator ....IDAHO
Alfonse D'Amato U.S. Senator ....NEW YORK

John C Danforth U.S. Senator ....MISSOURI
Thomas A Daschle U.S. Senator ....SOUTH DAKOTA
Herb Denenberg T.V.star, The Denenberg Investigative Report..........PENNSYLVANIA
E.V. DiMassa Jr. T.V. Producer, Senor Vice Pres. of King World Enterprises his credits include: The Mike Douglas Show; Regis & Kathy Lee Show; Hollywood Squares; Candid Camera and Inside Edition. Also created the best tasting recipe for Stuffed Artichoke Ernani ....CALIFORNIA
Dave Durenberger U.S. Senator ....MINNESOTA
Lauch Faircloth U.S. Senator .... NORTH CAROLINA
Dianne Feinstein U.S. Senator ....CALIFORNIA
Paul Jay Fink Associate Vice President Albert Einstein Healthcare Foundation.........PENNSYLVANIA
Kirk Fordice Governor of.......... MISSISSIPPI
Robert Gevjan Senior Computer Consultant, Bob is a computer genius, and keeps mine up and running.........PENNSYLVANIA
Phil Gramm U.S. Senator ....TEXAS
Charles E Grassley U.S. Senator ....IOWA
Amenda Gregory 1994 Junior State Champion.......... OKLAHOMA
Orrin G Hatch U.S. Senator ....UTAH
Walter Hickel Governor of.......... ALASKA
James M Jeffords U.S. Senator ....VERMONT
Melissa Johnson 1994 State Champion.......... OKLAHOMA
Paul Kanjorski Congressman .........PENNSYLVANIA
Nancy Landon Kassebaum U.S. Senator ....KANSAS
John F Kerry U.S. Senator .........MASSACHUSETTS
Bruce King Governor of.......... NEW MEXICO
Frank R Lautenberg U.S. Senator ....NEW JERSEY
Carl Levin U.S. Senator ....MICHIGAN
Joseph I Leiberman U.S. Senator ....CONNECTICUT
Harold B. Lipsius Owner of Universal Dist. one of the top 20 powerful people in the record business. His companies are a major factor in sales of recorded product.........PENNSYLVANIA
Annie Little 1994 State Champion.........OKLAHOMA
Mike Lowery Governor of ....WASHINGTON
Richard G Lugar U.S. Senator.........INDIANA
Connie Mack U.S. Senator.........FLORIDA
Harlan Mathews U.S. Senator ....TENNESSEE
Mitch McConnell U.S. Senator ....KENTUCKY
Jim McDermott Congressman ....WASHINGTON
Howard M Metzenbaum U.S. Senator ....OHIO

Robert Miller Governor of.........NEVADA
Gloria F Moppert my sister, a beautiful person..........PENNSYLVANIA
Benjamin Nelson Governor of ....NEBRASKA
Sam Nunn U.S. Senator ....GEORGIA
Joe Paterno Penn State Football coach,a living legend who coaches his team to win, and makes winners of the men he coaches..........PENNSYLVANIA
Jannika Percell 1994 SENIOR STATE CHAMPION.........OKLAHOMA
David H. Pryor U.S. Senator ....ARKANSAS
Harry Reid U.S. Senator ....NEVADA
John D Rockefeller IV U.S. Senator ....WEST VIRGINIA
William V Roth Jr. U.S. Senator ....DELAWARE
Jim Sasser U.S. Senator ....TENNESSEE
Grace Sayre truly loves this State ....OREGON
William Donald Schaefer Governor of.........MARYLAND
Edward T Schafer Governor of.........NORTH DAKOTA
Richard C Shelby U.S. Senator ....ALABAMA
Paul Simon U.S. Senator ....ILLINOIS
Allen K Simpson U.S.Senator ....WYOMING
Arlen Specter U.S. Senator .........PENNSYLVANIA
Fife Symington Governor of ....ARIZONA
Tommy G Thompson Governor of ....WISCONSIN
John W Warner U.S. Senator ....VIRGINIA
Pete Wilson Governor of.......... CALIFORNIA
Harris Wofford U.S. Senator .........PENNSYLVANIA
William H Zeliff Jr. Congressman ....NEW HAMPSHIRE

Appetizers

APPETIZERS
ANTIPASTO, PAGE 11
ARTICHOKE ERNANI, PAGE 10
ROASTED PEPPER RAINBOW, PAGE 12

BEVERAGES
LEMONADE, PAGE 13
WASSAIL, PAGE 9

SENATOR DAN COATS WASSAIL

COATS' FAMILY RECIPE

"THIS COLD WEATHER BEVERAGE IS ONE OF OUR WINTER FAVORITES THAT MY WIFE MARCIA AND I ENJOY."

WASSAIL
INGREDIENTS
4   cups of pineapple juice
4   cups of cider
1   cup of orange juice
1-1/2   cups of apricot nectar
1   6 inch cinnamon stick
1   teaspoon of whole cloves

DIRECTIONS
Combine all ingredients. Bring to a boil and simmer for 20 minutes. Strain before serving.
Makes 10 cups.

E.V. DI MASSA JR.
STUFFED ARTICHOKE ERNANI

STUFFED ARTICHOKE ERNANI

My favorite way to serve this is as an appetizer or in place of a salad, sometimes with mustard dip or melted butter.

INGREDIENTS:
- 1   fresh artichoke
- 1/2   cup of bread crumbs
- 1/2   teaspoon of parsley
- 1/2   teaspoon of basil
- 2   teaspoons of extra virgin olive oil
- 1/2   teaspoon of finely chopped garlic
- 4   stuffed green olives, chopped

DIRECTIONS:

Mix ingredients in bowl (cold). Prepare fresh artichoke for stuffing. Wash carefully, drain thoroughly and remove stem and all dark leaves to heart. Carefully separate leaves and place the mixture from center out, also between the leaves which will fan them out to resemble a flower. Place stuffed artichoke in pan with 1/2 inch of water and two teaspoons of olive oil, sprinkle with parsley. Do not allow to boil, cook only until leaves appear tender to the touch.

Serves 1

May add as many multiples as you like.

Here's a *Winner!*

Appetizers 10

JOE PATERNO SUE PATERNO'S ANTIPASTO

INGREDIENTS:
Dice or chop the following vegetables:
4 raw carrots
4 green peppers
2 large onions
1 stalk of celery
1 lb. fresh mushrooms
1 cauliflower (fresh)

DIRECTIONS:
In one cup of olive oil cook the above as follows:
Cook the carrots for five minutes, add onion, mushrooms and cauliflower for two minutes. Add celery and green peppers and cook for three minutes.
Mix the following in a large bowl.

2	small bottles of catsup (or 28 oz.)
3	teaspoons salt
2	bottles chili sauce (small)
2	teaspoons Accent
2	cloves garlic (optional)
	juice of two lemons.

Chop or break up the following to the sauce:

1	can tuna (drained)
1	lb. frozen king crab meat, defrosted and drained
2	jars artichoke hearts, drained
1/2	cup of pitted green olives
1/2	cup ripe olives

Add the cooked vegetables to the above. Mix everything together and let it marinate in the refrigerator for 24 hours. May be served hot or cold.

NOTE: A whole recipe makes at least three quarts.

HERBERT S. DENENBERG ROASTED PEPPER RAINBOW

This recipe was handed down from my mother, FANNIE, to my wife, NAOMI.

CAUTION: Unless portions are strictly controlled, you can eliminate the meal which is supposed to follow this appetizer.

As a child, I always thought the dish was strictly Rumanian (my mother was born in Rumania), until I discovered a few other ethnic groups, most notably the Italians, also specialized in this dish.

My favorite way to serve this is: chilled with bread.

INGREDIENTS:
6 large peppers (2 yellow, 2 red, 2 green)
2 small cloves of garlic
3 tablespoons of olive oil
   salt and pepper

DIRECTIONS:
1. Peel and mince cloves of garlic, and put to one side.
2. Wash and dry peppers.
3. Place peppers in a pan under the broiler until the skins become dark or charred on all sides.
4. Remove the pepper and place in a bag to cool.
5. When cool, remove the seeds, wash or peel away the charred material, and cut peppers into slices.
6. Put garlic, oil and seasoning (salt and pepper to taste) in a serving dish along with peppers and marinate for about 25 minutes before serving.
7. You may add vinegar and/or a little sesame oil, as another variation.

JOE FIORENTINO LEMONADE

LEMONADE
INGREDIENTS:
1   cup of sugar
1   cup of water

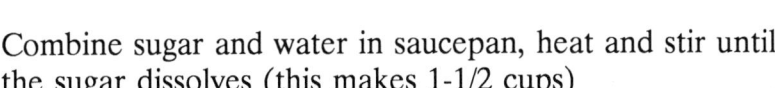

Combine sugar and water in saucepan, heat and stir until the sugar dissolves (this makes 1-1/2 cups)
1   cup of lemon juice (5 to 7 lemons)
3-1/2 cups of ice water
Add together the 1-1/2 cups of sugar water, 1 cup of lemon juice and the 3-1/2 cups of ice water. Serve in tall glasses filled with ice and garnish with a slice of lemon or mint leaf.
Serves 6.

Food Proverb
Don't bite the hand that feeds you.
What do you think this means? _____
_____
_____

HOW TO ADAPT GRANNY'S RECIPES TO HEALTHIER EATING

Substitution List to Healthier Eating. When your own recipe calls for:

WHOLE MILK (1 cup)
Use one cup of skim or nonfat milk plus 1 tablespoon of unsaturated oil.

HEAVY CREAM (1 cup)
Use one cup of evaporated skim milk or 1/2 cup of low-fat yogurt and 1/2 cup of low-fat cottage cheese.

SOUR CREAM
Use low-fat cottage cheese plus low-fat yogurt; ricotta cheese made from partially skimmed milk (thinned with yogurt or buttermilk, if desired); 1 can of chilled evaporated skim milk whipped with 1 teaspoon of lemon juice; or low-fat buttermilk or low-fat yogurt.

CREAM CHEESE
Use 4 tablespoons of margarine blended with 1 cup of low-fat cottage cheese. Add a small amount of skim milk if needed in blending the mixture. Add chopped chives or pimento and herbs and seasonings for variety.

BUTTER (1 tablespoon)
Use 1 tablespoon of polyunsaturated margarine or 3/4 tablespoon of polyunsaturated oil.

SHORTENING (1 cup)
Use 2 sticks of polyunsaturated margarine.

OIL (1 cup)
Use 1/4 cup of polyunsaturated margarine.

EGGS (1 egg)
Use 1 egg white plus 2 teaspoons of unsaturated oil or commercially produced cholesterol-free egg substitute according to package directions. Three egg whites for 2 whole eggs in baking recipes.

UNSWEETENED BAKING CHOCOLATE (1 ounce)
Use 3 tablespoons unsweetened cocoa or carob powder plus 1 tablespoon of polyunsaturated oil or margarine. Carob is sweeter than cocoa so reduce sugar by 1/4.

☐☐☐☐☐☐☐☐☐☐☐☐☐☐☐☐☐☐

Bread

BREAD
CORN BREAD, PAGE 16
MASSACHUSETTS CRANBERRY BREAD, PAGE 17
GARLIC BREAD, PAGE 22
WHOLE GRAIN HONEY BREAD, PAGE 18
GEORGIA PEACH BREAD, PAGE 15

SANDWICHES
HARD ROCK MINER'S HERO, PAGE 23

SENATOR SAM NUNN
GEORGIA PEACH BREAD

Georgia Peach Bread
- 3 cups fresh peaches, sliced
- 2 cups of all purpose flour
- 1/4 teaspoon salt
- 1 teaspoon ground cinnamon
- 2 eggs
- 1 cup of pecans, finely chopped
- 6 tablespoons of sugar
- 1 tablespoon of soda
- 1-1/2 cups of sugar
- 1/2 cup shortening
- 1 teaspoon vanilla

Place peaches and 6 tablespoons of sugar in blender and process until pureed (mixture should yield about 2-1/4 cups). Combine flour, baking soda, salt and cinnamon; set aside. Cream well 1-1/2 cups of sugar and shortening. Add eggs and mix well. Add peach puree and dry ingredients moistened, stir in nuts and vanilla. Spoon batter into 2 well greased and floured 9x5x3 loaf pans. Bake at 325 degrees for 55 to 60 minutes or until done. Cool 10 minutes in pan; then turn on rack and cool completely.

Yields: 2 loaves

SENATOR CHARLES E. GRASSLEY CORN BREAD

THE GRASSLEY FAMILY'S FAVORITE CORN BREAD RECIPE

INGREDIENTS:
1/4	cup of soft butter
1	cup of sugar
2	eggs
1	cup of corn meal
1-1/2	cups of flour
2	teaspoons of baking powder
1/4	teaspoon of salt
1-1/2	cups of sweet milk

DIRECTIONS:
Cream the butter and sugar. Add eggs and corn meal. Sift together flour, baking powder and salt. Add to creamed mixture alternately with sweet milk. Do not over beat. Put in greased 8 inch square or 9x13 pan. Bake at 375 degrees for 35 minutes or until done.

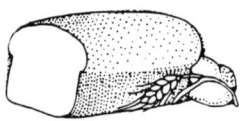

Food Proverb
Man does not live by bread alone
What do you think this
means _____

SENATOR JOHN F. KERRY MASSACHUSETTS CRANBERRY BREAD

"This is a delicious treat! My favorite way to serve this is with milk or tea, ENJOY."

INGREDIENTS:
- 1/4 cup of butter or margarine (softened)
- 1 cup of sugar
- 2 eggs
- 1 cup chopped Massachusetts cranberries
- 1/2 cup of water
- 1/2 teaspoon of vanilla
- 1-3/4 cups of flour (sifted)
- 1/2 teaspoon of baking soda
- 1-1/2 teaspoons of baking powder
- 1 teaspoon of salt
- 1/2 teaspoon of cinnamon
- 1/2 cup of chopped nuts

DIRECTIONS:
Cream the butter (or margarine) and sugar together in a large mixing bowl. Beat in the eggs with an electric mixer. Stir in the cranberries, water and vanilla. Sift the flour, baking soda, baking powder, salt and cinnamon together. Stir in with the batter. Add chopped nuts to the mixture. Pour into pan and bake at 350 degrees for 55 minutes. Serves 8

SENATOR PAUL SIMON HONEY WHOLE GRAIN BREAD

INGREDIENTS:

3	cups of white flour
2	pkgs. of active dry yeast
1-1/2	teaspoons of salt
1	cup of water
1	cup of cottage cheese
4	tablespoons of butter
1/2	cup of honey
2	eggs
2-1/2	cups of whole wheat flour
1/2	cup of regular rolled oats
2/3	cup of chopped walnuts or pecans

DIRECTIONS:

In a large bowl, combine 2 cups of white flour with yeast and salt. Heat water, cottage cheese, butter and honey until very warm (120-130). Add warm liquid and eggs to flour mixture. Mix well. Add whole wheat flour, oats and nuts, stir in the remaining white flour (add more if necessary). Knead until smooth and elastic. Let rise until double. Punch down and place in two greased 5-1/4x9-1/4x3 inch pans. Let rise about one hour. Bake at 350 degrees for 35 to 40 minutes. Remove from pans onto cooling rack. Brush tops with butter.

SENATOR JIM SASSER MARY'S BRAN MUFFINS

INGREDIENTS:
- 2 cups of bran (not bran cereal)
- 2 cups of sifted flour
- 2 teaspoons of baking soda
- 1/4 teaspoon of salt
- 3/4 cup of sugar
- 1 cup of raisins
- 1 cup of buttermilk
- 3 tablespoons of dark molasses
- 1/2 cup of vegetable oil
- 1 large egg, at room temperature

DIRECTIONS:
Lightly coat with nonstick cooking spray the inside of the muffin tins (1-1/2 inch deep) to accommodate about 15 muffins. Thoroughly blend together the bran, flour, baking soda, salt, sugar and raisins in a bowl. Whisk the buttermilk, molasses, oil and egg in a bowl, pour over dry ingredient and mix until well blended.

Fill each cup 3/4 full of batter and bake the muffins on the middle level rack at 325 degrees for 20 to 25 minutes or until a wooden pick inserted in the center withdraws cleanly.

Cool the muffins in the pan for one minute, then remove from the cooling racks.

SENATOR PAUL SIMON BRAN MUFFINS

INGREDIENTS:
1	cup of sugar or 1-1/2 cups of honey
2-3/4	cups of flour
1/2	teaspoon of salt
2-1/2	teaspoons of soda
2	eggs
3 or 4	cups of hard spring wheat bran (other bran will do)
2	cups of buttermilk
1	teaspoon of baking powder
1/2	cup of oil, sunflower is best
1	cup of boiling water
1	cup of raisins or chopped dates

DIRECTIONS:
Pour boiling water over dates or raisins and add soda. Mix together other ingredients, add cooled raisins and date mixture. Mix lightly, pour in muffin tins. Bake at 375 degrees for 20 minutes. This recipe should make 24 muffins.

GOVERNOR TOMMY G. THOMPSON OAT BRAN MUFFINS

I am pleased to share some of our favorite recipes. This Oat Bran recipe is a favorite of mine and Mrs. Thompson.

INGREDIENTS:
- 3 cups of flour
- 2 cups of bran cereal flakes
- 2 cups of oat bran
- 1 cup of brown sugar
- 1/2 teaspoon of salt
- 1 teaspoon of baking soda
- 2-1/2 cups of skim milk
- 2 egg substitutes
- 1/2 cup of melted margarine (cholesterol-free)

DIRECTIONS:
Grease two (12 muffin tins). Combine the first six ingredients in bowl. Add milk, eggs and margarine and stir until blended. May add walnuts, raisins or dates. Bake in a 400 degree oven for 15-20 minutes or until golden brown.
Makes 24 muffins.

JOE FIORENTINO GARLIC BREAD & ANCHOVY

GARLIC BREAD with ANCHOVY
INGREDIENTS:
1   loaf Italian bread
1   can of anchovy (or paste)
     garlic powder
     butter
     black olives, sliced

DIRECTIONS:
Slice one loaf of Italian bread into 1 inch thick slices, and butter lightly on one side. Sprinkle garlic powder on buttered area and place 1 anchovy (or anchovy paste) on top of butter and garlic. Place under broiler until starting to turn brown. Garnish with sliced black olives.

Food Proverb
Don't cry over spilt milk.
What do you think this means. _____

SENATOR HARRY REID HARDROCK MINER'S HERO

U.S. Senator Harry Reid grew up in the small dusty mining town of Searchlight, Nevada. His father was a hardrock miner, one of many who helped build the "SILVER STATE'S" economic base and it's reputation for hard working independence. Mining is still a major industry in Nevada, along with gaming and tourism. The HARDROCK MINER HERO, is a tribute to the tough minded individuals who carved an honest living from the land and helped settle the wild west.
The hint of Mesquite and Sage flavoring is intended to evoke the aroma and taste of the enticing desert Southwest.

INGREDIENTS:/DIRECTIONS:
1 large loaf of French Bread
deli-sliced roast beef
Monterey Jack cheese
lettuce
tomato
oil (add liquid mesquite flavoring)
vinegar
spices: add sage spice to oregano spice mix
Cut loaf of bread down center and combine ingredients in generous amounts.

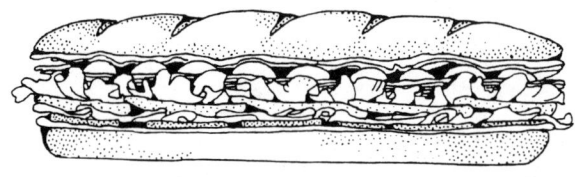

Breads/Sandwiches 23

HOW TO CARVE A TURKEY

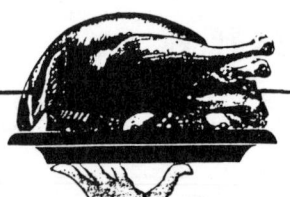

For a Perfect Turkey

1. Purchase ¾ to 1 pound of turkey per person.
2. Thaw safely in refrigerator in original wrapping. (Allow 24 hours for each 5 pounds of bird.)
3. Prepare stuffing, allowing ¾ cup of stuffing per pound of bird. A 12 pound turkey will hold approximately 9 cups of stuffing. Bake extra stuffing separately.
4. Take off plastic wrapping. Remove pouch of giblets and neck from cavity. Rinse turkey inside and out with cool water. Drain well.
5. Spoon stuffing into neck cavity and fold skin over securing with skewers or toothpicks.
6. Remove legs from stuffing clamp if it has one. Loosely stuff body cavity. Depending on brand of turkey, tie legs together with string or use stuffing clamp.
7. Place turkey breast-side up in large roasting pan. If desired, brush with oil or margarine.
8. Insert meat thermometer into center of thigh next to body. Be sure the thermometer is not touching bone. For a moist bird, cover with foil.
9. Roast at 325°F allowing about 20 minutes per pound. Turkey is done and most tender when thermometer reaches 180-185°F. Remove foil during the last half hour of roasting for a golden bird.
10. For best flavor and easy carving, remove turkey and let stand for 15-20 minutes.

CARVING A TURKEY

1. **Remove drumstick and thigh** — To remove drumstick and thigh, press leg away from body. Joint connecting leg to the hip will oftentimes snap free or may be severed easily with knife point. Cut dark meat completely from body by following body contour carefully with knife.

2. **Slicing dark meat** — Place drumstick and thigh on cutting surface and cut through connecting joint. Both pieces may be individually sliced. Tilt drumstick to convenient angle, slicing towards table as shown in illustration.

3. **Slicing thigh** — To slice thigh meat, hold firmly on cutting surface with fork. Cut even slices parallel to the bone.

4. **Preparing breast** — In preparing breast for easy slicing, place knife parallel and as close to wing as possible. Make deep cut into breast, cutting right to bone. This is your base cut. All breast slices will stop at this horizontal cut.

5. **Carving breasts** — After making base cut, carve downward, ending at base cut. Start each new slice slightly higher up on breast. Keep slices thin and even.

Remember, you'll get better results carving your turkey if you allow it to stand 20 minutes after you take it out of the oven.

Cakes/Cookies

FRESH APPLE CAKE, PAGE 31
NORWEIGIAN APPLE CAKE, PAGE 39
BLUEBERRY BUCKLE, PAGE 34
JOAN SPECTER'S CARAMEL PINEAPPLE, PAGE 32
CARROT CAKE, PAGE 26
CHOCOLATE CHEESECAKE, PAGE 40
COCONUT CAKE, PAGE 25
MAPLE SYRUP CAKE, PAGE 41
MISSISSIPPI MUD CAKE, PAGE 33
NANNY'S MOLASSES CAKE, PAGE 27
PENN STATE UNIVERSITY ORANGE CAKE, PAGE 28
CHOCOLATE PECAN CAKE, PAGE 37
CHOCOLATE STEAMED PUDDING, PAGE 29
YUM YUM CAKE, PAGE 38
ANN SIMPSON'S CHEESECAKE, PAGE 30
CHOCOLATE NUGGET, PAGE 36
COOKIES
BISCOCHITOS, PAGE 47
CHINESE CHEWS, PAGE 48
FRENCH MINT, PAGE 35
GRANDMOTHER MERRICK'S, PAGE 45
TOFFEE NUT BAR, PAGE 44
SCHAEFER'S WAFERS, PAGE 73
SOUR-CREAM SUGAR COOKIES, PAGE 44

GOVERNOR E. BENJAMIN NELSON COCONUT CAKE

COCONUT CAKE
INGREDIENTS:
1   Package Yellow Cup Cake Mix
1   Can Eagle Brand Sweetened Condensed Milk
1   Can Cream of Coconut
1   Carton Whipped Cream, Whipped

DIRECTIONS:
Bake cake according to the package directions. In a 9x12 inch greased pan, bake until done. When done, poke holes in cake with a fork. Pour the can of condensed milk and the can of cream of coconut over the cake. Let cool. Spread the whipped cream over the cake, then sprinkle with coconut flakes.

SENATOR CARL LEVIN CARROT CAKE

Carl Levin

INGREDIENTS:
- 1 cup of flour
- 3/4 cup of sugar
- 1 teaspoon baking powder
- 3/4 teaspoon of baking soda
- 1/2 teaspoon cinnamon
- 1/2 teaspoon of salt
- 5/8 cup of oil
- 2 eggs
- 1 cup of grated carrots
- 1 small can crushed pineapples (drained)
- 1/2 cup roughly chopped walnuts

DIRECTIONS:
Put all the ingredients in processor and mix 5 to 10 seconds. Add eggs and oil and mix for 30 seconds (will be very thick). Add the carrots and pineapple and mix through. Add nuts and mix only to distribute. Bake in greased pan about one hour at 350 degrees.

FROSTING
- 3oz. butter
- 1/2 teaspoon of vanilla
- 3oz. cream cheese
- 6oz. confectioners sugar (3 heaping tablespoons)

DIRECTIONS:
Process butter, cheese and vanilla for about 29 seconds. Add sugar and continue mixing. When cake is cold, pat all over.

The above recipe is made with a blender, however it can be adapted to a mixer.

CONGRESSMAN BILL P. BAKER NANNY'S MOLASSES CAKE

Bill Baker

This is a favorite recipe in our family and has been passed down from generation to generation.

INGREDIENTS:
- 1 cup of white sugar
- 1/2 cup of molasses
- 1/2 cup of shortening
- 2 cups of flour
- 2 teaspoons of cinnamon
- 1 teaspoons of ginger
- 2 eggs, beaten
- 1 cup of raisins
- 1 cup of water, hot

DIRECTIONS:
Beat all the above ingredients together. Add one cup of hot water in which two teaspoons of baking soda have been dissolved.
Put into a 9x11 inch greased pan and bake at 325 degrees for 25 to 35 minutes.

JOE PATERNO PENN STATE UNIVERSITY ORANGE CAKE

ORANGE CAKE from the desk of JOE PATERNO, Penn State University.

INGREDIENTS:
- 1   large Florida Orange
- 1   cup of raisins
- 1/3   cup of walnuts
- 1/2   cup of vegetable shortening
- 1   cup sugar
- 2   large eggs
- 2   cups of flour
- 1   teaspoon of baking soda
- 1   teaspoon of salt
- 1   cup of milk

DIRECTIONS:
Squeeze 1/3 cup of juice from orange; (reserve for Orange-Nut Topping). Remove any seeds from orange; place unpeeled orange, raisins and nuts in a blender or food processor; process until finely ground. Set aside in large mixer bowl; cream shortening and sugar; beat in eggs. Combine flour, baking soda and salt. Add to creamed mixture alternately with milk. Fold orange-raisin mixture into batter. Spread batter into greased and floured 13x19x2 inch baking dish. Bake in a preheated 350 degree oven 40 to 50 minutes. Cool 10 minutes.

ORANGE-NUT TOPPING:
- 1/3   cup of sugar
- 1/4   cup of chopped walnuts
- 1   teaspoon of ground cinnamon

Drizzle reserved 1/3 cup orange juice over warm cake. Combine sugar, walnuts and cinnamon; sprinkle over cake. Garnish with whole walnuts and orange slices if desired.
Yield: 20 servings.

CONGRESSMAN WILLIAM H. ZELIFF JR. CHOCOLATE STEAMED PUDDING CAKE

Sydna Zeliff

Recipe from Bill and Sydna Zeliff, Jr. This is a fourth generation recipe from SYDNA'S family and has always been the special favorite desert of the Zelif family.

CREAM TOGETHER:
- 1 tablespoon of butter
- 1/2 cup of sugar* then add
- 1 egg
- 1 square unsweetened chocolate melted* add alternately
- 1/2 cup of milk* flour mixture consisting of:
- 1 cup of flour
- 1/2 teaspoon baking soda
- 1 teaspoon of cream of tartar* COOK in a steam pan covered with a cloth for 45 minutes.

SAUCE MIX TOGETHER:
- 2/3 cup of butter
- 2 cups of 10X powdered sugar
- 1 teaspoon of vanilla
- 4 egg yolks

The passion for Chocolate

BEAT UNTIL STIFF AND DRY:
- 4 egg whites *FOLD IN:

Stiff eggs whites to rest of the ingredients for sauce and cook in a double broiler over boiling water until sauce is hot. Approximately 15 minutes.
Serve Sauce over cake.

SENATOR ALAN K. SIMPSON ANN SIMPSON'S BLENDER CHEESECAKE

This recipe is from my lovely wife, ANN, for Blender Cheesecake. It is a dandy one and has always been one of my favorites.

Pre-heat oven 350 degrees

CRUST:
1   cup of graham crackers
     (or 12 graham crackers)
1/2 stick of melted butter

Mix and press in pie plate.

FILLING:
4   3 oz. packages of cream cheese (softened)
2   eggs
3/4 cup of sugar

Blend well, until creamy. Be careful not to overbeat, pour into crust. Bake in the 350 degree oven for 20 minutes. Remove from oven and cool for 5 minutes.

TOPPING:
1/2 pint of sour cream
3   tablespoons of sugar
1   teaspoon of vanilla

Mix and pour over cheesecake. Spread around. Put back in oven for 10 minutes, covered. Remove and cool, then refrigerate.

Serves 8-10
Top with frozen strawberries.

SENATOR HARLAN MATHEWS FRESH APPLE CAKE

THIS IS ONE OF MY ALL TIME FAVORITES. THE RECIPE IS TRIED AND TRUE; I HOPE YOU ENJOY IT AS MUCH AS I DO.

Harl Mathews

1/2	cup of canola oil
2	cups of sugar
3	eggs
2-1/2	cups of all purpose flour
1/2	teaspoon of salt
3/4	teaspoon of soda
1	tablespoon of baking powder
1	tablespoon of cinnamon
1	tablespoon of cloves
3	cups of diced apples (York or Granny Smith preferred)
1-2	cups of pecans and/or walnuts
2	tablespoons of rum

Blend the canola oil, sugar and eggs. Then add and mix well, the all purpose four, salt, soda, baking powder, cinnamon and cloves. Add and stir well the diced apples, nuts and rum. Pour into tube pan that has been buttered and floured. Cook for 1 hour 15 minutes, at 325 degrees.

Food Proverb
And Apple doesn't fall far from the tree. What do you think this means. _____

Cakes/Cookies 31

SENATOR ARLEN SPECTER MRS. JOAN SPECTER'S CARAMEL PINEAPPLE CAKE ROLL

Mrs. Joan Specter's recipe for Caramel Pineapple Cake Roll

2	cans crushed pineapple, drained
1/2	cup of dark brown sugar
3/4	cup cake flour
1	teaspoon of baking powder
1/2	teaspoon of salt
4	large eggs, separated
3/4	cup of sugar
2	teaspoons of vanilla
1	teaspoon of grated lemon rind.

Butter well a 10x15 inch jelly roll pan. Spread drained fruit evenly over bottom of pan and sprinkle with brown sugar. Sift flour with baking powder and salt. Beat egg whites until foamy and add 3/4 cup of white sugar gradually, beating until stiff. Beat yolks into stiffened whites, and add vanilla and lemon rind.

Sprinkle flour over all and gently fold in. Spread batter evenly over the pineapple and brown sugar. Bake in a pre-heated oven at 375 degrees for 18 to 20 minutes. Turn upside down on a damp towel and sprinkle lightly with confectioner's sugar. Roll up in a towel and cool. Remove towel when cool, place cake on platter and ice.

ICING

1	cup of heavy cream
3	tablespoons of confectioner's sugar

Beat heavy cream with sugar until stiff.

SENATOR JAMES M. JEFFORDS MAPLE SYRUP CAKE

IT IS A PLEASURE TO SHARE WITH YOU AN OLD FAVORITE VERMONT RECIPE OF MINE.

MAPLE SYRUP CAKE
INGREDIENTS:

1/2	cup shortening
1/2	cup white sugar
2	eggs (beaten lightly)
1	cup maple syrup
1/4	cup water
2-1/2	cups cake flour
1/4	teaspoon soda
2	teaspoons baking powder
1/2	teaspoon ginger

James M Jeffords

DIRECTIONS:
Cream the shortening, gradually add sugar. Add the eggs beaten without separating the white and yolks. Add maple syrup and water, then the flour which has been sifted, measured and sifted again with the ginger, soda and baking powder added. Bake in a tube loaf pan about 50 minutes at 325 degrees. Cover with maple icing and decorate with walnut halves.

Food Proverb
You can't have your cake and eat it too
What do you think this
means _____

GOVERNOR TOMMY G. THOMPSON BLUEBERRY BUCKLE

This recipe of Blueberry Buckle is Mrs. Thompson's Favorite.

INGREDIENTS:
- 2 cups of sifted flour
- 2 teaspoons of baking powder
- 1/2 teaspoon of salt
- 1/4 cup of soft butter
- 1 cup of sugar
- 1 egg
- 1/2 cup milk
- 2 cups of fresh or frozen blueberries.

DIRECTIONS:
Sift together flour, baking powder and salt. Cream butter and sugar until light and fluffy. Add the egg and milk and beat well. Add flour, baking powder and salt and stir until blended. Add blueberries, spread mixture into 9 x 13 inch pan.

TOPPING
- 1/2 cup of brown sugar
- 1/3 cup of flour
- 1/4 cup of soft butter
- 1/2 teaspoon of cinnamon

Cream together butter and sugar. Combine flour and cinnamon and add to creamed mixture. Stir until crumbly. Sprinkle over blueberry buckle and bake 35-45 minutes at 350 degrees.

SENATOR ORRIN G. HATCH FRENCH MINT

Enclosed is a copy of my favorite dessert recipe, French Mint. I would like to share this recipe with everyone. I think they will enjoy this one. A delicately mint-flavored frozen dessert.

French Mint
INGREDIENTS:
- 4 squares 1 oz.* unsweetened chocolate
- 1 cup of soft butter
- 2 cups of confectionery sugar
- 4 eggs
- 1 teaspoon of vanilla
- 1 teaspoon of peppermint extract
- chopped nuts

DIRECTIONS:
Melt chocolate. Cool and set aside. Using an electric beater, beat butter while gradually adding sugar (about 15 minutes). Add cooled melted chocolate. Beat 5 minutes more. Beat in eggs one at a time. Mix in vanilla and peppermint extract.

Sprinkle chopped nuts on bottom of 24 paper cupcake holders in cupcake pan. Fill each cupcake holder half full. Sprinkle more nuts on top.

Freeze for at least 3 hours.

*Can substitute 6 oz. package of chocolate chips.

GOVERNOR BOB MILLER CHOCOLATE NUGGET

This is one of Governor Miller's favorite recipes.

INGREDIENTS:
- 6 ounces Nestles Chocolate Chips
- 1 egg
- 1/2 teaspoon of vanilla
- 3/4 cup of milk
- dash salt

DIRECTIONS:
Mix ingredients and microwave on high for 2 minutes. Put in blender for one minute. Pour into little cups and refrigerate until set.

Food Proverb
A way to a man's heart is through his stomach
What do you think this means _____

SENATOR ARLEN SPECTER JOAN SPECTER'S CHOCOLATE PECAN CAKE

Arlen Specter

1	stick of butter
1/2	cup of granulated sugar
1/2	cup of shredded coconut
2/3	cup of chopped pecans
1/2	cup of semisweet chocolate morsels
1	tablespoon of milk
1	cup of flour
1/2	cup of dark brown sugar
1-1/2	teaspoons of baking powder
1/4	teaspoon of salt
1/2	teaspoon of vanilla extract
1/3	cup of water
1	egg

Preheat oven to 350 degrees. Melt 1/2 stick of butter in a small saucepan. Remove from heat. Stir in brown sugar, coconut, pecans, chocolate morsels, milk and blend well. Spread the mixture in the bottom of a 9-inch round cake pan. Set aside. Stir together the flour, sugar, baking powder and salt in mixing bowl. Add the remaining 1/2 stick of butter, the vanilla, water and egg and beat until batter is thoroughly blended and smooth. Pour over the coconut pecan mixture, bake for about thirty minutes or until a toothpick inserted in the center of the cake comes out clean. Cool in the pan for about 5 minutes, then turn onto a serving plate, coconut pecan mixture on top. Serve the cake warm or cold with vanilla ice cream.

The passion for Chocolate

GLORIA F. MOPPERT
YUM YUM CAKE

YUM YUM CAKE is the perfect name for this cake, and over the last 48 years has been served hundreds of times. Every family function by four generations. YUM YUM CAKE is still the favorite dessert of everyone. I was so pleased when asked by my brother to contribute the CHRISTMAS DINNER MENU for his book. I suggested that we share the Yum Yum cake recipe with everyone. This is not only a great granny recipe, but a four generation tradition in the Fiorentino family. I guess you could call it a great, great Granny recipe. ENJOY.

INGREDIENTS:
- 2 cups of sugar
- 1/2 cup of butter
- 1 box of raisins, large size
- 1/4 teaspoon of salt
- 2 teaspoons of nutmeg
- 1/4 teaspoon of all-spice
- 2 teaspoons of cinnamon
- 2 cups of cold water
- 1/2 cup of cold coffee
- 3 cups of sifted flour
- 2 teaspoons of baking soda

DIRECTIONS:
Combine all ingredients above into a large (3 quart size) saucepan. Stir. Cook for 3 minutes then let mixture cool, set aside. Dissolve 2 teaspoons of baking soda into 1/2 cup of cold coffee. Add this to the cold mixture and fold in 3 cups of sifted flour. Mix gently and pour into a 10 inch Tube pan. Bake in a 350 degree oven for 1 hour or longer.

GRACE and BILL SAYRE REPRESENT OREGON with NORWEGIAN APPLE CAKE *Grayce Sayre*

We moved to Oregon to be near my son and family, and discovered the most beautiful place in the world. The mountains are breath taking and the Evergreens so pretty. People here are very friendly and helpful. It is home to us now. We are pleased to represent our State with these recipes. I first made the Apple cake recipe in 1968 and now with our Oregon apples it never tasted better.

NORWEGIAN APPLE CAKE
INGREDIENTS:
- 2 eggs
- 9 ounce caster sugar (1 cup, 2 tb. white sugar)
- 3-3/4 ounces butter (just short of 1/4 lb.)
- 1/2 pint of top milk (1/2 cup of milk)
- 6-1/2 ounces plain flour (1 cup 2 tb.)
- 2 rounded teaspoons baking powder
- 3-4 pounds of cooking apples

DIRECTIONS:
Whisk eggs and sugar together until whisk leaves a trail when lifted out of mixture. Put butter and milk in a pan, bring to boil and stir into egg and sugar mixture. Fold in sifted flour and baking powder until no lumps. Pour mixture into buttered floured roasting pan. Peel, core, quarter and slice apples, arrange over batter. Sprinkle with 1/4 cup sugar. Bake cake at 400 degrees for 20-25 minutes. When cooked let cool in tin.

Food Proverb
An Apple a day keeps the doctor away
What do you think this means _____

Cakes/Cookies 39

GOVERNOR FIFE SYMINGTON CHOCOLATE CHEESECAKE

CHOCOLATE CHEESECAKE

INGREDIENTS:

1	pkg (9 oz.) chocolate wafers, crushed
1/2	stick butter
12	oz. semi-sweet chocolate
1/2	cup of strong hot coffee
2	pkgs (8 oz.) cream cheese, softened
4	eggs
1	cup of sugar
2	teaspoons of vanilla
	whipping cream

The passion for Chocolate

DIRECTIONS:
Melt butter and stir in chocolate wafers. Pat mixture into 8 inch springform pan on the side and bottom. Melt chocolate with coffee and mix well. Beat cream cheese, eggs, sugar and vanilla together. Stir in chocolate mixture, and pour into pan. Bake at 325 degrees for 55 minutes. Turn off oven, but don't remove the cheesecake for 2 to 3 hours. DON'T PEEK. Serve with whipped cream.
Serves 12.

GOVERNOR KIRK FORDICE MISSISSIPPI MUD CAKE

The enclosed recipe is one of my favorites-MISSISSIPPI MUD CAKE.
Mississippians can's get enough of this mud.
MISSISSIPPI MUD CAKE
DIRECTIONS:

- 1   cup of butter
- 1/2   cup of cocoa
- 2   cups of sugar
- 4   eggs, slightly beaten
- 1-1/2 cups of pecans, chopped
- 1-1/2 cups of flour
- pinch salt
- 1   teaspoon vanilla
-       Miniature Marshmallows
-       Chocolate Frosting

DIRECTIONS:
Melt butter and cocoa together. Remove from heat. Stir in sugar and beaten eggs, mix well. Add flour, pinch of salt, nuts and teaspoon of vanilla. Spoon batter into greased and floured 13x9x2 inch pan. Bake at 350 degrees for 35 to 45 minutes. Sprinkle marshmallows on top of hot cake and then cover with chocolate frosting.

CHOCOLATE FROSTING
- 1   box of powdered sugar
- 1/2   cup of milk
- 1/3   cup of cocoa
- 1/2   stick of butter

DIRECTIONS:
Combine sugar, milk cocoa butter and mix until smooth. Spread on the hot cake.

SENATOR DAVE DURENBERGER MINT STICK BROWNIES

MINT STICK BROWNIES
- 2 squares of chocolate
- 1/2 cup of butter
- 2 eggs well beaten
- 1 cup sugar
- 1/4 teaspoon of peppermint flavoring
- 1/2 cup of sifted flour
- 1/8 teaspoon salt
- 1/2 cup of chopped nuts
- 1/4 teaspoon of baking powder

Melt chocolate and butter on top of double boiler. When melted add sugar and beaten eggs. Add sifted flour, baking powder and salt. When melted add peppermint flavoring and nuts. Pour into 8x10 inch pan. Bake at 350 degrees for 25 minutes (or until done). Cool.

MINT STICK BROWNIES FROSTING AND GLAZE
FROSTING:
- 2 tablespoons of butter (soft)
- 1 cup of sifted powdered sugar
- 1 tablespoon of cream
- 1/2 teaspoon of peppermint flavoring
- green food coloring.

Mix until creamy and spread on cooled brownies.

GLAZE TOPPING:
- 1 sq. of baking chocolate
- 1 tablespoon of butter

Combine and melt on double boiler. Blend well and drizzle over brownies. Carefully tip pan to cover surface. Refrigerate to set.

SENATOR SAM NUNN COLLEEN NUNN'S DOUBLE CHOCOLATE BROWNIES

These recipes are particular favorites of my family, the recipe for Georgia Pecan Pie is my favorite, my wife COLLEEN'S favorite is this one DOUBLE CHOCOLATE BROWNIES.

INGREDIENTS:
- 3/4 cup of all-purpose flour
- 1/4 teaspoon of salt
- 1/4 teaspoon of baking soda
- 1/3 cup of butter
- 2 tablespoons of water
- 3/4 cup of sugar
- 1 12 oz. package of semi-sweet chocolate chips
- 1 teaspoon of vanilla
- 2 eggs
- 1/2 cup of chopped pecans

The Passion for Chocolate

DIRECTIONS:
In a small bowl combine flour, baking soda and salt. Set aside. In a small saucepan combine butter, sugar and water; bring just to a boil. Remove from heat. Add 6 oz. chocolate chips and vanilla. Stir until melted and the mixture is smooth. Transfer to a large bowl. Add eggs, one at a time, beating after each addition. Gradually blend in flour mixture. Stir in remaining 6 oz. chocolate chips and nuts. Pour into 9 inch greased square baking pan. Bake at 325 degrees for 40 to 45 minutes.

SENATOR DAN COATS' SOUR-CREAM SUGAR COOKIES

These are our son, ANDREW'S, favorite cookies. This recipe belongs to VERA COATS, Senator Dan Coats' mother.

INGREDIENTS:
- 1 cup butter
- 1 cup of sugar
- 1 egg
- 1 cup of sour cream
- 1 teaspoon of vanilla
- 2 cups of flour
- 1 teaspoon of soda
- 1/2 teaspoon of salt
- 1/2 teaspoon of nutmeg

Cream the butter and sugar together. Add the egg, sour cream and vanilla.

Sift all the dry ingredients together and add to the first mixture.

CHILL FOR AT LEAST 2 HOURS - OR OVERNIGHT.

Place on greased cookie sheet by large spoonfuls, place a few raisins in the middle of each cookie, if you like, and sprinkle with sugar. Bake at 400 degrees for 10 minutes.

SENATOR WILLIAM S. COHEN GRANDMOTHER MERRICK'S SOFT MOLASSES COOKIES

I AM ENCLOSING ONE OF MY FAMILY'S FAVORITE RECIPES. I HOPE IT WILL BE A SUITABLE ADDITION TO YOUR COLLECTION.

GRANDMOTHER MERRICK'S SOFT MOLASSES COOKIES

INGREDIENTS:
- 1/3 cup of shortening
- 1/2 cup of boiling water
- 1 teaspoon of salt
- 3/4 cup molasses
- 1/2 cup granulated sugar
- 2-1/2 cups sifted all-purpose flour
- 2 teaspoons baking powder
- 1/2 teaspoon soda
- 1 teaspoon ginger
- 1 teaspoon cinnamon

DIRECTIONS:
Place the shortening in bowl. Pour in boiling water and add salt. Stir molasses and sugar. Add unbeaten egg and beat well. Sift flour; measure and sift together with baking powder, soda, ginger and cinnamon. Stir into mixture. Drop by spoonful onto greased cookie sheet. Bake at 375 degrees for 12 to 15 minutes.

GOVERNOR EDWARD T. SCHAFER TOFFEE NUT BAR

This is one of my favorite recipes, TOFFEE NUT BAR. The best way to serve this is as a dessert.

INGREDIENTS and DIRECTIONS:
1/2   cup of shortening
1/2   cup of brown sugar
Cream these ingredients together.
Stir in:
1   cup of regular flour; press mixture down in a 13x9 inch greased pan, and bake at 350 degrees for 10 minutes.
Add:
2   eggs, beat well and add
1   cup of brown sugar
1   teaspoon of vanilla and beat well
2   tablespoon of flour and
1   teaspoon of baking powder
Then add:
1   cup of chopped nuts (either pecans or walnuts) and
1   cup of coconut
Spread over baked cookie-like mixture, then bake at 300 degrees for an additional 25 minutes. Cut into bars and sprinkle with confectioners sugar and ENJOY.
Serves 24.

Edward T Schafer

GOVERNOR BRUCE KING BISCOCHITOS

INGREDIENTS:
- 2 cups of Morrell lard
- 1 cup of sugar
- 3 eggs
- 3 teaspoons of baking powder
- 1/2 teaspoon of salt
- 1 teaspoon of vanilla
- 1/4 cup of orange juice
- 5 cups of flour

DIRECTIONS:
Cream lard, sugar and eggs. Add vanilla and orange juice, then mix in baking powder, flour and salt.

Mixture can be put into refrigerator overnight or made right away. Can be made with cookie cutter or with pastry gun. If made with gun, dip them in sugar and cinnamon after they are baked. If cut with cookie cutters, dip them before baking.

Bake at 400 degrees for 12-15 minutes.

Bruce King

CONGRESSMAN JAMES E. CLYBURN CHINESE CHEWS

CHINESE CHEWS
EMILY CLYBURN'S Recipe for Chinese Chews, is a family favorite. The number of portions from this recipe are (21 fingers) or 25 squares.
I use cookie sheets and cut mixture into 2x2 inch squares.

INGREDIENTS:
1/2 lb. butter or margarine (2 sticks)
1/2   cup of white sugar
1-2/3   cup of soft flour
3   eggs, separated
1   cup of firmly packed brown sugar
1/2   cup of coconut
1/2   cup of nuts, chopped (walnuts or pecans)

DIRECTIONS:
Cream sugar with 1/2 lb. of butter or margarine. Blend in the flour and pat mixture onto a greased cookie sheet and bake in moderate 350 degree oven for 15 minutes.
Beat egg yolks until thick, gradually add brown sugar while beating constantly. Add coconut and nuts. Fold in stiffly beaten egg whites and spread this mixture over the baked mixture.
Return to oven and bake for 20-25 minutes at 350 degrees.
Cut into 2x2 inch squares or fingers while warm, and dust with brown sugar. Eat and be merry!

SENATOR DIANNE FEINSTEIN SAN FRANCISCO CHEESE PIE

SAN FRANCISCO CHEESE PIE
INGREDIENTS:
Crust:
1   cup of crushed graham crackers
3/4   cup of melted butter
4   tablespoons of sugar
Combine all ingredients and line in a pyrex pie pan.

Filling:
4   cubes of cream cheese
1/2   teaspoon of vanilla
2   beaten whole eggs
1/2   cup of sugar
Beat eggs, add vanilla and sugar, then add the cream cheese cubes one at a time. Pour in prepared crust. Bake in oven at 375 degrees until lightly browned.

Topping:
3/4   pint of sour cream
2   tablespoons of sugar
1/2   teaspoon of vanilla
Beat until smooth.

Bake, on pie, for additional five minutes.
ENJOY!!!

COOKING & RESTAURANT TERMS
(and what they mean)

A LA....In the style of, a way of doing.
A LA CARTE....Individually ordered selections unlike the complete meal with appetizer, salad, main course and desert for one price.
AL DENTE....To the tooth (pasta) cooked as to be firm when eaten.
A LA KING....chopped up food usually poultry served in cream sauce.
A LA MAISON....in the style of, a way of doing of the house.
A LA MODE....topped with ice cream usually on (pie or cake) deserts.
AMANDINE....made or served with almond nuts.
AU GRATIN....with a crust, topped with cheese or bread crumbs.
AU JUS....roasted natural meat juices.
BASTE....moisten during cooking or before with drippings or other liquids.
BEAT....to thoroughly mix ingredients using spoon or mixer.
BISQUE....cream soup with fish or pureed vegetables.
BLANCH....to immerse foods in boiling water.
BOIL....heated water to 212 degrees or to cook foods in boiling water.
BONE....to remove all bones (fillet)
BREAD....dip or cover with crumbs before cooking.
BROIL....cook by direct heat from flame or electric broiler.
BUTTERFLY....to section in half usually large shrimp and thick fillet steaks.
CANAPE....small toast or cracker covered with food spread.
CARTE DU JOUR....(paper) menu of the day.
CORE....remove the core or the center.
CREPE....(French pancakes) very thin pancakes.
CREPE SUZETTE....thin French pancakes rolled in sauce and set aflame.
DOT....spatter drops of butter on food before cooking.
DREDGE....to coat with flour.
DU JOUR....of the day, as in soupe Du jour.
FILLET....bones have been removed or to remove bones.
FLAMBE....deserts soaked with liquor and set aflame.
FROMAGE....French for cheese
GARNISH....to decorate with color foods, as parsley, olives, lemon slices etc.
GAZPACHO....a soup served cold with fresh vegetables.
HORS D'OEUVRES....food served before meals as appetizers.
HUSK....to remove outer leaves covering corn as in corn husker.
JULIENNE....food cut in long thin strips.
MORNAY....a cheese flavored white sauce.
MULL....heat with spices.
RAGOUT....a seasoned stew of meat and vegetables.
SAUTE....to cook, to brown in hot melted butter or oil.
SKIM....to spoon off fat from top of liquid.
SOUFFLE....eggs whipped to froth then baked till puffy.
STEEP....soak in hot liquid to draw color and flavor.
THICKEN....mix in flour or corn starch to add density.
WHIP....to beat repeatedly, as in eggs whites.

MEAT

CAROL'S BLACK BEAN & SAUSAGE, PAGE 58
BAKED BEANS, PAGE 64
LITE & LEAN BEEF BROIL, PAGE 51
BURGOO, PAGE 62
CHILI CON CARNE, PAGE 56
GRAMM'S AWARD WINNING CHILI, PAGE 55
MEATBALLS, PAGE 54
PEPPER PORK CHOPS, PAGE 57
BROILED PORK CHOPS, PAGE 60
SAUSAGE SOUFFLE, PAGE 54
SWEET & SOUR SPARERIBS, PAGE 53
MONTANA EASY TACO MEATBALLS, PAGE 61
SOUTH DAKOTA TACO SALAD, PAGE 59
TOMATO BEEF RECIPE, PAGE 52

SENATOR LARRY E. CRAIG LITE AND LEAN BEEF BROIL

Lite and Lean Beef Broil from SUZANNE CRAIG.
Enclosed is one of Suzanne and my favorite meat recipes. This was served July 8, 1993 at the Wedding Luncheon of Suzanne and Larry Craig in Midvale, Idaho.

INGREDIENTS:
1-1/2 lbs. beef sirloin steak, top round, flank or brisket.
Marinade:
1/2   cup soy sauce
1/4   cup water
1 oz.   (2 tablespoons) lemon juice
1 oz.   (2 tablespoons) honey
1   teaspoon instant minced onion
1/4   teaspoon garlic powder

Method:
Combine marinated ingredients in a non-metal pan, add beef and turn to coat.
Marinate beef for 24 to 48 hours in refrigerator.
Broil beef to desired doneness, do not overcook; best served medium rare.
To serve:
Slice beef across the grain into thin slices. Sprinkle with sesame seeds. Serves four to six.

SENATOR & MRS. HARRIS WOFFORD TOMATO BEEF RECIPE

Harris Wofford (signature)

TOMATO BEEF RECIPE

May be partially prepared ahead, or may be cooked at the table.

2-3	pounds of sirloin, top round or flank steak
1/2	pound of fresh mushrooms
1	large onion (or 2 small)
1	large green pepper (or 2 small)
4	tomatoes
1-1/2	teaspoons of cornstarch
2	tablespoons of sherry
1/2	cup of water
2-1/2	tablespoons of soy sauce*
2	tablespoons of sugar

Slice steak into strips 2 inches long and 1 inch thick, cutting across the grain. Slice the mushrooms. Cut the tomatoes, green pepper and onion into large chunks. In hot skillet (in electric skillet set at 390 degrees), add a tablespoon of oil and saute the mushrooms. When the mushrooms are partially cooked, add the onions and cook these quickly. Push both of these to the side of the pan and add the slices of steak and two pieces of tomato. Mash tomato to release tomato flavor to the sauce. Brown the steak quickly and sprinkle on the sugar, sherry and soy. Add green peppers and remaining tomatoes. Make a paste of cornstarch and water and add that to the pan. Cook three more minutes and serve over hot rice.

* If Chinese shoyu sauce is used, decrease the shoyu to 2 tablespoons and increase the sugar to 2-1/2 tablespoons.

SENATOR DANIEL K. AKAKA SWEET/SOUR SPARERIBS

Daniel K Akaka

SWEET/SOUR SPARERIBS
Marinate overnight 5 lbs. pork butt, cut into 1-1/2 inch pieces.

MARINADE:
1/2	cup shoyu
1	teaspoon garlic salt
1/4	teaspoon pepper
1/2	teaspoon of aji
	ginger, garlic

Flour soaked pieces and brown. Bring sauce to a boil and add pork. Simmer for 1 hour or until pork is tender.

SAUCE:
2	cups of sugar
1	cup of vinegar
1-1/2	cups of water
1/4	cup of shoyu
2	teaspoons of salt
1	teaspoon of aji (optional)

You may use pineapple chunks for a garnish. Use the juice from the pineapple chunks and add it to the sauce.

SENATOR HANK BROWN MEATBALLS

INGREDIENTS:
1 lb. hamburger meat
1 large diced onion
2 tablespoons of flour
   salt and pepper (to taste)
1 can (pound) tomatoes

DIRECTIONS:
Mix ingredients above, (except tomatoes) with a fork or your fingers, roll into balls, a little larger than golf balls, brown over slow heat, turning often.
Add the can of tomatoes, first strain pulp of tomatoes through a strainer. Simmer at least one full hour.
Serve over mashed potatoes.

SENATOR PAUL SIMON SAUSAGE SOUFFLE

SAUSAGE SOUFFLE
6 slices of white bread, remove crust and cube
1 lb. of port sausage, brown and drain
1 cup mild cheddar cheese, shredded
8 eggs
1 teaspoon of salt
1 teaspoon of dry mustard
2 cups of milk
Grease 9 x 13 glass pan, put layer of bread, then sausage. Beat eggs, add milk, salt and mustard, pour over bread. Top with cheese and cover with plastic wrap overnight. Bake 45 minutes at 350 degrees. This recipe serves eight.

SENATOR PHIL GRAMM
SENATOR GRAMM'S AWARD WINNING CHILI

SENATOR GRAMM'S AWARD WINNING CHILI

2 lbs. of meat, part ground and part cut into sugar cube size.
1 small onion, minced; or 1 heaping tablespoon of dehydrated onion. Brown and drain, if necessary.

Add:

2	(8 oz.) cans of tomato sauce
2	(8 oz.) cans of water
4	tablespoons chili powder
1/2	teaspoon salt
2	teaspoons of paprika (optional)
1	tablespoon of ground cumin (optional)
1/2-1	teaspoon red pepper (optional)
2	cloves of garlic, minced
2-3	tablespoons of flour

Cook 1-2 hours. Add: 2-3 tablespoons of flour. Cook 15 minutes.

ENJOY.

SENATOR JOHN C. DANFORTH - JACK'S HOMEMADE CHILI CON CARNE

3-1/2 pounds of top round, cut in 1/2 inch cubes
5 tablespoons of oil
2 cups of coarsely chopped onion
4 cloves of garlic, minced
4 tablespoons of chili powder
1-1/2 teaspoons of oregano
1-1/2 teaspoons of ground cumin
1 teaspoon of crushed red pepper
2 cups of beef broth
1 can (1 pound 3 oz.) whole tomatoes
1 6 oz. can of tomato paste
3 cans of kidney or chili beans
1 tablespoon of salt; 1 teaspoon of sugar
1-2 tablespoons of yellow cornmeal

Pat the meat dry with paper towels. Heat 3 tablespoons of oil in a large heavy pot. When hot add the meat all at once. Sear it until all the pieces are lightly browned, about 3 to 4 minutes. Use spoon and turn meat constantly. Transfer meat to bowl and add the remaining 2 tablespoons of oil to the pot. Add the onion and garlic and saute until the onion is wilted but not browned. Stir in the chili powder, oregano, cumin, and red pepper; mix well until the onions are coated. Add the broth, can of tomato (juice and all), tomato paste, salt, and sugar, mixing well. Break up tomatoes with the back of spoon. Pour out a portion of juice from the meat bowl and return the meat to the pot, cover and simmer for one hour. Then uncover and simmer for 40 to 50 minutes, add beans. Cook, cover and refrigerate overnight. To serve, bring slowly to a boil and simmer until heated through. Thicken with cornmeal to desired consistency.

SENATOR ALFONSE D'AMATO - PEPPER PORK CHOPS

INGREDIENTS:
- 6 medium pork chops
- 3 green bell peppers, sliced
- 3 to 4 vinegar peppers
- 2 medium potatoes
- 4 tablespoons, corn oil
- 1/4 cup vinegar (from pepper jar)

DIRECTIONS:
Peel and cube potatoes and boil until slightly tender. In heavy skillet, add corn oil and pork chops to brown. Remove pork chops after browning, and add sliced bell peppers. Cook peppers until slightly tender.
Add pork chops, potatoes; cooking for about 5 minutes.
Add sliced vinegar peppers and vinegar to skillet mixture. Cover and let cook over medium heat for 5 to 10 minutes.
Salt and pepper to taste.
Yield: 4 servings.

SENATOR CAROL MOSELEY-BRAUN
CAROL'S BLACK BEAN AND SAUSAGE

Carol Moseley Braun

CAROL'S BLACK BEAN AND SAUSAGE

3	cans black beans (goya canned)
1-1/2	large onion chopped
1	large green pepper chopped
3/4	teaspoon of garlic
1/4	teaspoon of cumin (ground)
8	oz. olive oil (extra virgin)
1	teaspoon of vinegar
1	tablespoon of bacon grease
1	lb. sausage

Saute green pepper with bacon grease; then add onion; let brown; add garlic; then drain beans; add olive oil; cumin. Add meat (cooked); simmer at low heat; add vinegar for about 5 minutes then mash beans to achieve thickness, let settle overnight (optional).

NOTE: You may substitute sausage with other meats such as ham, pork chops, smoked meat or even smoked turkey.

SENATOR THOMAS DASCHLE - SOUTH DAKOTA TACO SALAD

Tom Daschle

South Dakota Taco Salad makes a main meal especially delicious on a hot day, as this is really a beef dish and a salad all in one. A real SOUTH DAKOTA tradition on the plains!

INGREDIENTS:

1 lb.	ground beef
2	package taco seasoning mix
1	head of lettuce-chopped or torn
1	can red kidney beans, drained
	sliced tomatoes
1	green pepper, diced (optional)
8 oz.	shredded cheddar cheese
1	bottle Russian dressing

DIRECTIONS:

Brown meat until done (or according to taco seasonings mix directions). Cool beef after adding seasoning. Cut up lettuce, tomatoes, just as you would for a garden salad. Mix all with cooled beef, beans and cheese. Carefully mix in Russian dressing. When ready to serve, crush approximately 8 taco shells (or use crushed taco flavored chips such as Doritos) and carefully fold the pieces into the salad for a nice crunchy taste.

SENATOR LAUCH FAIRCLOTH - BROILED PORK CHOPS

BROILED PORK CHOPS

1/2	cup of tomato juice
2	tablespoons of cider vinegar
1	tablespoon of Worcestershire sauce
1	teaspoon of prepared mustard
1/2	teaspoon of sugar
1/4	teaspoon of salt
1/4	teaspoon of garlic salt
1/4	teaspoon of hot sauce
4	(1 inch thick) pork chops

Combine the first eight ingredients, and set aside.

Place pork chops on lightly greased rack of broiler pan; brush with tomato juice mixture. Broil 4 to 5 inches from heat 15 minutes, turning once and brushing occasionally with sauce. Yield: 4 servings.

Note: To braise pork chops, brown on both sides in 1 tablespoon of vegetable oil in a large nonstick skillet; drain. Return pork chops to skillet, add tomato juice mixture. Bring mixture to a boil; cover, reduce heat, and simmer for 15 minutes.

SENATOR CONRAD BURNS - MONTANA QUICK AND EASY TACO MEATBALLS

Here is a good and quick way to enjoy TACO MEATBALLS. The key to the recipe is to use home grown MONTANA BEEF.

INGREDIENTS:
2	lbs. hamburger meat
1/2	chopped onion
2	slightly beaten eggs
1	package of taco mix
	salt (to taste)
	pepper (to taste)
	garlic (to taste)

DIRECTIONS:
Mix all ingredients above into small size meatballs and place on cooking sheet.
Bake at 400 degrees for 15 minutes. ENJOY!
My favorite way to serve this is with Tacos.

Serves 4.

SENATOR MITCH McCONNELL BURGOO

Mitch McConnell

BURGOO is a stew-like dish from Kentucky served often at large gatherings of family and friends. The Derby is a particularly popular occasion to serve this dish, which is a meal in itself. It takes two days to prepare, but do not let that scare you the final product is worth the wait. This is best made when fresh vegetables are at their peak, but frozen vegetables and canned tomatoes can be used when necessary. It freezes well.

			salt
1	4 to 5 lbs. hen	1-1/2	teaspoons of black pepper
1	lb. of beef stew meat	1/2	teaspoon of cayenne
1	lb. of veal stew meat	6	onions, finely chopped
4	large beef or knuckle bones	2	green peppers finely chopped
2	cups of thinly sliced celery	1	medium turnip finely diced
1	can (10 oz.) tomato puree	8-10	tomatoes, peeled and chopped
4	quarts of water		
1	red pepper pod		

1   (tablespoon of each):lemon juice, Worcestershire sauce, sugar,
2   (cups of each):shelled   fresh butterbeans, celery, cabbage, fresh okra, corn, (6 ears)
1/2   unpeeled lemon, seeded

If you make this in two parts, on successive days, it is not such a chore. Put the hen, stew meat, veal stew meat, knuckle bones, tomato puree, water, pepper pod, salt, Worcestershire, sugar, black pepper, and cayenne in a roaster, bring to a boil and simmer slowly, covered, for about 4 hours. Let cool and strain. Cut chicken and meat fine, remove all skin, bone and gristle. Scissors are good for this job. Return to stock and refrigerate. The following day lift off half the fat, add all vegetables except corn and okra, sauteeing first the onions and green peppers in a little bacon fat or butter. Simmer slowly for an hour, covered. Uncover, add okra and cook another hour or until thick. Cut corn twice, scraping to get the milk. Add this along with the lemon and additional seasonings. If you finish the cooking in the oven, it will eliminate stirring and watching. Cook uncovered, at 300 degrees for about 2 hours until the consistency of a thick stew. This will make a gallon. If made before hand, reheat in the oven to insure against scorching. Serve in mugs and sprinkle with chopped fresh parsley.

Meat 62

Take a Taste Tour of America
What's Cookin' in the U.S.A.

GOVERNOR E. BENJAMIN NELSON - BAKED BEANS

INGREDIENTS:
3 lbs. of Italian sausage
2 large onions, chopped
2 large green peppers, cut into rings
3 large cans of Van de Kamp Pork and Beans, drained
2 teaspoons of liquid smoke
3 12 oz. bottles chili sauce
1 32 oz. jar of molasses (use 2/3 of it)
4 teaspoons of horseradish
3 teaspoons prepared mustard

DIRECTIONS:
Cut sausage into small chunks and cook until brown. Remove from pan, add chopped onion. Cook onion until transparent. Mix sausage and onion with remaining ingredients, with the exception of the green pepper rings. Pour mixture into a 3 quart casserole dish. Arrange the green pepper rings on top. Bake at 350 degrees for 1-1/2 hours.

Serves 20.

Pasta

ANN & FIFE'S LASAGNA, PAGE 67
SPAGHETTI WITH GARLIC AND OIL, PAGE 65
SPAGHETTI WITH CLAM SAUCE, PAGE 66

JOE FIORENTINO SPAGHETTI WITH GARLIC, OIL AND ANCHOVY *Joe Fiorentino*

Spaghetti with garlic, oil and anchovy. As you can see, I use a lot of garlic when I cook. This dish is a favorite of mine.

INGREDIENTS
1   lb. of spaghetti
2   tablespoons of parsley, chopped
4   cloves of garlic, chopped
5 quarts of water
2   cans of Anchovy in oil (2 ounce) each
     salt
1/2 cup of olive oil

DIRECTIONS:
Fill large pot with the 5 quarts of water, put in a pinch of salt and two teaspoons of oil. Bring to a boil and add spaghetti. Cook for 8-10 minutes. Meanwhile in a separate pan saute the garlic (use oil from the 2 cans of anchovy); if not using anchovy in this recipe; use 8 teaspoons of oil. When garlic is golden brown add parsley, anchovy and 1/2 cup of olive oil. Stir and cook for 3 minutes. Mix with cooked spaghetti and serve.
Note: If you choose not to use the 1/2 cup of olive oil, use 2 cups of water from pot with cooked spaghetti before discarding water.

ROBERT & JANET GEVJAN SPAGHETTI WITH CLAM SAUCE

This recipe can be modified as to the amount of individuals being served. A red or white clam sauce can be used.

INGREDIENTS:
- 4 crushed cloves of garlic
- 2 four ounce cans of chopped clams with clam juice
- 1/4 cup of olive oil
- 3/4 teaspoon of oil
- pinch salt

DIRECTIONS:
Add garlic and oil to fry pan and saute until light brown. Add chopped clams and juice and heat. In a separate large pot, fill with water and add 3/4 teaspoon of oil and a pinch of salt. Bring to boil and add spaghetti. Cook 8 minutes or until desired consistency is reached. Drain the spaghetti, put in large serving bowl, add the clam sauce and enjoy.

To make the red clam sauce, add some tomato paste when you are making up the sauce.

> Food Proverb:
> If you can't take the heat stay out of the kitchen.
> What do you think this means?

GOVERNOR FIFE SYMINGTON - ANN AND FIFE'S LASAGNA

Our recipe for lasagna is definitely a crowd pleaser, and the Turkey sopa has a uniquely southwest taste. I hope you enjoy the LASAGNA, TURKEY SOPA and CHOCOLATE CHEESECAKE recipes as much as my family and I do.

INGREDIENTS:
- 2 lbs. of extra ground beef
- 1 large onion, chopped
- 1 clove of garlic, minced
- 6 bay leaves (remove after cooking)
- 1 12 oz. can of tomato paste
- 2 12 oz. cans of water
- salt and pepper (to taste)
- 12 lasagna noodles

DIRECTIONS:
Cook above ingredients together slowly, at least one hour (about #3 on electric range). Twenty minutes before meat is done, cook twelve lasagna noodles as directed on the package. Rinse in cold water. Keep in water until ready to use.

In glass dish (16x11x2) place six noodles. On top of the noodles put half of the sauce,
- 1 cup of cottage cheese
- 1/4 cup fresh grated parmesan cheese and
- 1/2 lb. grated mozzarella cheese.

Start with the noodles and repeat.

Cover with foil, place on cookie sheet and bake at 350 degrees for 45 minutes. Let rest at least 20 minutes before serving.

Serves 12

Behind the Safe Food Label

Store & Thaw Safely

Refrigerate or freeze meat and poultry the minute you get home from the store. Most foodborne bacteria can only grow slowly if at all at 40° F, a safe refrigerator temperature. Freezer temperatures of 0° F stop bacterial growth.

Thawing food on the counter is risky because foodborne bacteria can multiply rapidly at room temperatures. Thaw in the refrigerator or microwave. When you thaw food in the microwave, cook it right away.

The 'Whys'

Cook Thoroughly

Cooking food all the way through is the single best protection you have against foodborne illness. Of course, you don't want tough, dried-out meat.

Use the temperatures in the chart (right) for safe, juicy results.

When you're not using a thermometer, look carefully at meat products before you serve them. Ground meat and poultry should be gray in the middle. For whole birds and poultry pieces, the juices should run clear.

Safe Handling Instructions

This product was prepared from inspected and passed meat and/or poultry. Some food products may contain bacteria that could cause illness if the product is mishandled or cooked improperly. For your protection, follow these safe handling instructions.

Keep refrigerated or frozen.
Thaw in refrigerator or microwave.

Keep raw meat and poultry separate from other foods.
Wash working surfaces (including cutting boards), utensils, and hands after touching raw meat or poultry.

Cook thoroughly.

Keep hot foods hot. Refrigerate leftovers immediately or discard.

For larger sized red meats like roasts, the surface should be well browned, but they may look slightly pink in the middle. However, if you have cut into the meat with a knife (scoring) or poked it with a fork to tenderize it, exposing the interior to bacteria, cook the meat to medium or well done.

Why can larger, unpierced cuts of red meat be pink in the center while ground meats can't? Ground meats receive so much grinding that surface bacteria can get mixed into the center. Therefore they must be cooked all the way through. Larger cuts of red meat do not usually present those risks.

Don't Spread Bacteria In the Kitchen!

Keep raw meat, poultry and their juices away from other food.

- For example, don't chop salad vegetables on a cutting board where you've just trimmed raw meat or poultry.
- At the grill, take a clean platter out to serve "cooked meat, not the "bloody" platter you took them out to the grill on.

ALWAYS wash your cutting board, utensils, counter, sink and hands with hot, soapy water after contact with raw meat or poultry.

Handling

Handling Leftovers

Bacteria and other pathogens are always ready to endanger your food. Perishable food must be kept HOT (140° F and above) or COLD (40° F or lower) to keep them from taking over.

Refrigerate leftovers within 2 hours after cooking or serving. Divide leftovers into small refrigerator dishes for safe, quick cooling. Discard anything left out too long.

Product	Fahrenheit
Fresh Beef, Veal, Lamb	
Ground products like hamburger (Prepared as patties, meat loaf, meatballs, etc.)	160
Roasts, steaks and chops	
Medium Rare	145
Medium	160
Well done	170
Fresh Pork	
All cuts including ground product	
Medium	160
Well done	170
Poultry	
Ground chicken, turkey	165
Whole chicken, turkey Medium, unstuffed	170
Well done	180
Whole bird with stuffing (Stuffing must reach 165°)	180
Poultry breasts, roasts	170
Thighs, wings	Cook until juices run clear
Ham	
Fresh (raw)	160
Fully cooked, to reheat	140

Pastry/Pies

GRANNY'S APPLE PIE, PAGE 72
SAN FRANCISCO CHEESE PIE, PAGE 49
CHEESE PIE, PAGE 70
ICE CREAM PIE, PAGE 70
LEMON MOUSSE, PAGE 71
MARY'S BEST LEMON PIE, PAGE 69
CREAMY PEACH PIE, PAGE 74
GEORGIA PECAN PIE, PAGE 71

SENATOR JIM SASSER - MARY'S BEST LEMON PIE

1-1/2 cups of sugar
2 tablespoons of sugar
1/4 teaspoon of cream of tartar
4 eggs, separated
1/4 teaspoon of butter (for greasing the pie plate)
1 tablespoon grated lemon rind
3 tablespoons of lemon juice
2 cups of heavy cream

SIFT...together 1 cup of the sugar and cream of tartar. Beat egg whites until stiff. Slowly fold in the sugar mixture and beat until well blended. Butter the sides and the bottom of a 9-inch pie plate. Scrape the meringue mixture into the pie plate, building it up around the edges to fashion a shell. Place in a pre-heated 275 degrees oven and bake 1 hour. Remove and place on rack to cool.
BEAT... egg yolks until light and lemon colored. Add the 1/2 cup of sugar. Add lemon rind and lemon juice and beat to blend. Cook in the top of a double boiler until thickened, stirring constantly. Remove from heat and let cool.
WHIP...half of the cream until stiff and fold into the lemon filling. Pour this into the meringue shell. Chill until the filling is set.
WHIP...the remaining cream with the remaining 2 tablespoons of sugar and spoon on the top of the filling.
CHILL...uncovered for 24 hours.

SENATOR PAUL SIMON CHEESE PIE

Paul Simon

8 oz.	package of cream cheese (softened)
1	unbaked, 8 inch Graham cracker crust
1/2	cup of sugar
1	tablespoon of lemon juice
1/2	teaspoon of vanilla
2	eggs
1	cup of sour cream
2	tablespoons of sugar

Beat cheese until fluffy. Gradually blend in 1/2 cup of sugar, lemon juice, vanilla and a dash of salt. Add eggs one at a time, beating well. Pour filling into crust. Bake at 325 degrees for 25 to 30 minutes, until set. Combine the rest of the ingredients. Spoon over top of pie and bake for 10 minutes longer. Chill.

SENATOR NANCY LANDON KASSEBAUM ICE CREAM PIE

The Passion for Chocolate

3	squares of semi-sweet chocolate
1/3	stick of butter
2	cups of Rice Krispies
	ice cream
1	10 inch pie plate

Nancy Landon Kassebaum

Melt 3 semi-sweet chocolate with the 1/3 stick of butter. Mix in the 2 cups of Rice Krispies. Press into buttered pie plate.

Fill with the ice cream such as coffee crunch and top with grated chocolate. Freeze. Take out of freezer about 1/2 hour before serving.

SENATOR SAM NUNN GEORGIA PECAN PIE

These recipes are particular favorites of my family, the recipe for GEORGIA PECAN PIE is my favorite, and my wife COLLEEN'S favorite is chocolate brownie recipe.
GEORGIA PECAN PIE
- 1-1/4 cups sugar
- 1/2 cup light corn syrup
- 1/4 cup butter or margarine
- 3 eggs, slightly beaten
- 1 cup coarsely chopped pecans
- 1 teaspoon vanilla

Pastry for 9-inch pie
Preheat oven to 350 degrees; meanwhile combine sugar, syrup and butter in 2-quart saucepan. Bring to boil on high, stirring constantly until butter is melted. Remove from stove and gradually add hot syrup to eggs; stir all the while. Add pecans to mixture and cool to lukewarm. Add vanilla. Pour into pie shell and bake for 40 to 45 minutes.
Serves 6 to 8

SENATOR PAUL SIMON LEMON MOUSSE

Pour 2 cups of boiling water over 6 oz. package of lemon Jello and stir until dissolved. Add two 7 oz. bottles of lemon lime carbonated drink (like 7 Up). Add grated rind of 1 lemon and the juice. Chill until slightly thick (about 2 hours). Beat until foamy. Fold 2 cups of heavy cream whipped. Turn into a two quart souffle dish, chill until firm. Serve with fresh berries, slightly sweetened.
Serves 8.

CONGRESSMAN JIM McDERMOTT - GRANNY'S APPLE PIE

I am pleased to provide you with a copy of my mother's famous apple pie. It is my favorite recipe my mother MRS. ROSEANNA W. McDERMOTT makes.

INGREDIENTS:
- 2 crusts
- 2 cups of flour
- 3/4 cup of margarine or butter
- 1/4 cup of ice cold water
- 1/2 teaspoon of salt

Put flour and margarine in food processor and process just seconds until the mixture is the size of peas. Gradually add water while processor is running. Process until a ball forms, just takes seconds. Remove ball from processor and divide in half. Wrap each half in wax paper or plastic wrap. Refrigerate 1/2 hour or longer. Prepare apples, when complete, roll out dough on lightly floured board and fit one piece into pan.

APPLE FILLING

Peel and thinly slice 6 apples or enough to make 6 cups, put into a 3 quart mixing bowl and add 3/4 cups of sugar, 2 tablespoons of cornstarch, and 1 teaspoon of cinnamon. Gradually mix until apples are coated. Fill pie crust in pan. If apples are not tart enough, add a tablespoon of lemon juice and lemon rind. Dot top of filling with bits of 1-1/2 tablespoon of butter and cover with upper crust. Prick the top crust to release the steam and flute around edges. Protect fluted edges with aluminum foil. Bake pie for 15 minutes at 450 degrees and then 35 to 45 minutes at 350 degrees. The last 15 minutes remove foil from fluted edges so it can brown.

GOVERNOR WILLIAM DONALD SCHAEFER SCHAEFER'S WAFERS

Since it is an honor to be the GOVERNOR OF THE GREAT STATE OF MARYLAND, naturally, my favorite food is SEAFOOD, particularly when it is fresh from our Chesapeake Bay.

It is my pleasure to enclose as requested a recipe for one of MARYLAND'S BEST SEAFOOD DISHES, STEAMED CRABS.

Also I have enclosed my very own SCHAEFER WAFERS RECIPE which are very delicious COOKIES.

INGREDIENTS:
- 2 egg whites
- 1/3 cup of sugar
- 1/3 cup of sugar (again)
- 1/2 teaspoon of vanilla
- 1 6 ounce package of Toll House Chocolate Chips

DIRECTIONS:
Beat two egg whites, which are at room temperature, until stiff. Add 1/3 cup of sugar and beat three minutes. Add another 1/3 cup of sugar and beat for three more minutes. Add 1/2 teaspoon of vanilla. Fold in one 6 ounce package of Toll House Chocolate Chips. Drop by teaspoon onto cookie sheet.

Place in oven pre-heated to 375 degrees. Count to ten. Turn off oven. Leave cookies in oven overnight.

Makes fifty.

The passion for Chocolate

SENATOR DAVE DURENBERGER CREAMY PEACH PIE

WINNER OF THE BRAHAM, MINNESOTA BEST PIE RECIPE CONTEST*

INGREDIENTS:

1	package (3 ounces) peach gelatin
3/4	cup of boiling water
1	pint of peach ice cream
1	cup of cold milk
1	package of vanilla instant pudding
1/2	cup of Cool Whip
1	baked 8 inch pie shell

DIRECTIONS:
Dissolve gelatin in boiling water. Add ice cream. Stir until melted. Combine milk and pudding mix. Add to gelatin mixture. Whip until fluffy. Fold in whipped topping. Spoon mixture into pie shell. Chill for 2 hours. Serve with fresh peaches, strawberries or raspberries. Makes 8 inch pie.

* Custard and cream category

Poultry

BROCCOLI-CHICKEN CASSEROLE, PAGE 80
CHICKEN PARMESAN, PAGE 81
CHICKEN CUTLET ALA RUSSE, PAGE 78
CHEESY CHICKEN ENCHILADAS, PAGE 82
CHICKEN ENCHILADA CASSEROLE, PAGE 86
CHICKEN FAJITAS, PAGE 80
ANNIE'S LITTLE CHICKEN ROLL-UP, PAGE 88
ORIENTAL CHICKEN SALAD, PAGE 85
CHICKEN SCALLOPINI, PAGE 79
KOREAN CHICKEN, PAGE 75
MRS. COVERDELL'S CHICKEN, PAGE 83
MRS. TIPPER GORE'S CHICKEN, PAGE 77
DOVE ON THE GRILL, PAGE 84
TURKEY SOPA, PAGE 89
DEEP FRIED CAJUN TURKEY, PAGE 76
GRILLED TURKEY PITA POCKETS, PAGE 87

SENATOR DANIEL K. AKAKA - KOREAN CHICKEN

INGREDIENTS:
BATTER:
5   lb. bag of chicken (cup up)
1/2   cup flour
1   tablespoon of salt
SAUCE: (mix)
1   stalk of green onion, chopped
1/2   cup of shoyu
6   tablespoons sugar
1   clove garlic, chopped
1   teaspoon sesame oil
1   small red pepper, chopped (optional)

DIRECTIONS:
Salt chicken and let stand overnight in refrigerator. Roll chicken in flour and fry. After frying, dip chicken into sauce and serve.

SENATOR JOHN BREAUX CAJUN DEEP FRIED TURKEY   *John Breaux*

I am pleased to share my favorite and my family's favorite recipes. CAJUN DEEP FRIED TURKEY, Grandma Daigle's Rice Dressing, and Seafood Gumbo. All of the enclosed recipes are from the cajun country of Louisiana where I was born. I hope everyone enjoys them as much as we do.

INGREDIENTS:
4 oz. of liquid garlic
4 oz. of liquid onion
4 oz. of liquid celery
1 tablespoon of red pepper (cayenne)
2 tablespoons of salt
2 tablespoons of Tabasco
1 oz. of liquid crab boil or 1 tablespoon of Old Bay SEASONING:
1 poultry or meat injector
1 defrosted and cleaned 10-12 lbs. Turkey
5 gallons peanut oil

DIRECTIONS:
Saute the first seven ingredients until the salt and pepper are dissolved. Fill the injector and inject turkey at breast, wings, drumsticks, thighs and back. Allow to marinate 24 hours in refrigerator or ice chest. Use a ten gallon pot for frying. Bring peanut oil to 350 degree temperature and fry the turkey for 38 to 42 minutes. Turkey should float to surface after 35 minutes, and you should cook an additional 5 to 7 minutes.

***You may want to tie turkey legs with 1/2 inch cotton ropes to be able to remove from frying pot when done. The cooking of fried turkey should be done outdoors. Extreme caution should be taken when placing the turkey into the hot oil.

VICE PRESIDENT AL GORE - MRS. TIPPER GORE'S SPICED ROASTED CHICKEN

The Gore family recipe for Spiced Roasted Chicken is one of my favorites. I hope you enjoy it, too. Bon Appetit!

1	(3-1/2 lbs.) Chicken
1	tablespoon margarine; 2/3 cup of marsala
	MUSHROOM STUFFING:
2	tablespoons of olive oil
1	onion, fine chopped
1	teaspoon of garam marsala
4	oz. button, brown or chestnut mushrooms, chopped
1	cup of coarsely grated parsnips
1	cup of coarsely grated carrots
1/4	cup minced walnuts
2	teaspoons of chopped fresh thyme
1	cup of fresh white bread crumbs
1	egg, beaten
	salt and pepper to taste

TO GARNISH: Thyme and watercress sprigs
TO SERVE: Seasonal vegetables

Preheat oven to 375F (109C). Prepare Stuffing: In a large saucepan, heat olive oil; add onion and saute 2 minutes or until softened. Stir in garam marsala and cook 1 minute. Add mushrooms, parsnips and carrots; cook, stirring 5 minutes. Remove from heat; stir in remaining stuffing ingredients. Stuff and truss chicken. Place breast down, in roasting pan; add 1/4 cup of water. Roast 45 minutes; turn chicken breast up and dot with margarine. Roast about 45 minutes or until a meat thermometer inserted in thickest part of thigh (not touching bone) registers 185F (85C). Transfer to platter; keep warm. Pour off and discard fat from roasting pan; add marsala to remaining cooking juices, stirring to scrape up any browned bits. Boil over high heat 1 minute to reduce slightly; adjust seasoning. Remove skin and carve chicken. Garnish with thyme and watercress sprigs. Serve with stuffing, flavored meat juices and seasonal vegetables. Makes 4 servings.

SENATOR JOHN D. ROCKEFELLER IV
CHICKEN CUTLETS ALA RUSSE

Here's a *Winner!*

A favorite recipe from
The Honorable & Mrs. John D. Rockefeller IV
U.S. Senator, West Virginia

CHICKEN CUTLETS ALA RUSSE
Serves 8

2 lg	Chicken breasts	1/2-C	All purpose flour
1/4-tsp	Nutmeg	1 1/2-C	Bread crumbs
5 Tbl	Melted butter	1 lg	Egg
1-Tbl	water	1-tsp	Vegetable oil
6-Tbl	Butter		Salt and pepper

1. Chill your mixing bowl in the freezer while you remove the skin and bones from the chicken breasts. Finely chop the chicken meat or put through a grinder using a fine blade. You should have 1-1/2 cups of ground meat. If your market has chopped chicken meat you could save yourself the trouble -- turkey could also be substituted.
2. Add the meat to the chilled bowl and add the nutmeg, salt and pepper to taste and the 5-Tbl of melted butter. Beat well and chill in the freezer (do not freeze).
3. Season the 1/2-cup of flour with salt and pepper. Beat the egg with water in a small bowl and set aside. Take two pie pans and put the flour in one and the bread crumbs in the other. Now you have the three items lines up -- flour, egg, and bread crumbs. Have a piece of waxed paper next to the bread crumbs to put the dipped cutlet on.
4. Divide the chicken into 8 balls and flatten to 1/2-inch thick. Shape into a cutlet. Dip each in the flour, then the egg, and finally into the bread crumbs. Press the crumbs into the meat gently. When all 8 cutlets are done place them into the refrigerator.
5. At this time make your Paprika Sauce and keep warm. The recipe for the sauce follows.
6. In a heavy skillet heat the 6-Tbl of butter and 1-tsp of vegetable oil. When very hot carefully add the cutlets. Cook until golden brown on one side and turn and brown the other side.
7. Arrange on a hot platter and spoon some of the Paprika Sauce over the cutlets and keep hot or serve immediately.

Paprika Sauce

3-Tbl	Butter	3 med	Tomatoes
3-Tbl	Onion, finely chopped	2-Tbl	Sour cream
1/4-C	All purpose flour		Salt and pepper
1-Tbl	Paprika		

1. Peel the tomatoes and coarsely chop. You should have approximately 3-1/2 cups. Finely chop the onion for 3-tablespoons.
2. Melt two tablespoons of butter in a skillet. Add the onion and simmer until transparent and soft, do not brown. Stir in the flour and paprika, then stir in the tomatoes and add salt and pepper. Simmer fifteen minutes, stirring frequently. Stir in the sour cream. Swirl in the remaining butter by rotating the pan gently. Taste and correct with salt and pepper. Serve hot.

Jay Rockefeller

SENATOR ALFONSE D'AMATO - CHICKEN SCALLOPINI

CHICKEN SCALLOPINI

INGREDIENTS:

1	package of chicken cutlets (6)
3	tablespoons of butter
1/2	cup of corn oil
1/2	clove garlic, finely chopped
1/4	teaspoon, rosemary
1/4	teaspoon, oregano
1/4	cup of fresh lemon juice
1/4	cup of chopped fresh parsley
1	small can of sliced mushrooms

DIRECTIONS:
Heat butter and oil in heavy skillet over medium flame. When hot, add chicken cutlets and brown. When cutlets are brown, add finely chopped garlic, rosemary, oregano, lemon juice and salt and pepper to taste. Cover immediately. Let simmer for about 2 to 3 minutes. Add mushrooms. Cover again and let cook for 10 to 15 minutes. Before serving, add chopped fresh parsley. Yield: 3 servings.

SENATOR JIM SASSER CHICKEN FAJITAS

INGREDIENTS:
- 3-4   Boneless chicken breasts
- 1   stick of butter or margarine
- 1/2   teaspoon of garlic powder
-     juice of one lemon
-     salt & pepper
- 1   tablespoon of cooking sherry
- 3   tablespoons of teriyaki sauce

Jim Sasser

DIRECTIONS:
In a skillet, melt butter and stir in the garlic powder, lemon juice, salt and pepper, sherry and teriyaki sauce. Simmer 2 to 3 minutes, stirring frequently to blend the ingredients. Cut chicken into strips and add to the skillet. Cook until well done. Remove from skillet and roll up in warm flour tortillas, along with sauteed onion, green pepper strips, salsa, guacamole, and or sour cream.

SENATOR & MRS. CONNIE MACK BROCCOLI-CHICKEN CASSEROLE

- 2   packages of frozen broccoli
- 4   chicken breasts or (2) tuna size cans of chicken
- 1   package of Hollandaise sauce
- 1   can cream of chicken soup
- 2/3   cup of milk
- 2   tablespoons of white wine

Connie Mack

DIRECTIONS:
Cook broccoli. Brown chicken breasts in butter. Mix and pour the remainder of ingredients over the top. Cover and bake at 350 degrees for 20 minutes.

SENATOR FRANK R. LAUTENBERG - CHICKEN PARMESAN

CHICKEN PARMESAN

1 1/2-2	lbs. boneless breast of chicken
1 jar	favorite tomato sauce
2	eggs*
1	teaspoon of water
	seasoned bread crumbs
8 oz.	shredded mozzarella cheese
2	tablespoons of olive oil

Clean chicken breasts thoroughly, remove any fat. Pound breasts to 1/2 inch thickness with kitchen mallet. Set aside. Mix eggs and water in shallow dish. Dip chicken in egg mixture and then dredge through the bread crumbs. Be sure to fully coat the chicken.

Coat the bottom of the frying pan with olive oil and heat pan being careful not to overhead. Place coated cutlets into pan and cook until thoroughly done (about two minutes on each side).

Once thoroughly cooked, top with mozzarella cheese and cover with sauce. Place cover on pan and heat until cheese is melted and sauce is hot.

Serve with your favorite pasta and garlic bread.

* Can substitute egg whites if watching cholesterol

MELISSA JOHNSON 1994 A-OK COOK-OFF SENIOR CHAMPION STATE OF OKLAHOMA - CHEESY CHICKEN ENCHILADAS

2	cups Tyson chicken, cooked and shredded
1/4	cup green onions, chopped
1	clove of garlic, pressed
4	tablespoons of Braum's butter
1	can (4 ounces) diced green chilies
1/4	cup of J-M Farms mushrooms, chopped
1/2	teaspoon of dried oregano leaves
3	tablespoons Shawnee Mills all-purpose flour
2	cups of chicken broth
1/2	cup of low fat Farm Fresh sour cream
1	can (2-1/4 ounces) sliced black olives, drained
8	Orbit flour tortillas

1-3/4 cups Braum's Colby Jack cheese

For Garnishings:

3	cherry tomatoes; 3-4 J-M mushrooms, sliced
5	jalapenos; 2 sprigs cilantro
1	jar (16 ounces) Maria-Rae's salsa

Saute onion and garlic in butter. Stir in chicken chilies (reserve tablespoon for garnish) mushrooms, olives and oregano. Heat thoroughly. Set aside in saucepan, melt 2 tablespoons of butter. Stir in flour. Cook for 1 minute. Gradually stir in broth. Cook until slightly thickened. Add 1/2 cup of cheese. Add sour cream. Remove from heat. Stir 1/2 cup of the sauce in chicken mixture. Dip tortillas in chicken broth and spread 1/4 cup of sauce in bottom of baking dish. Spread each tortilla with sour cream sauce. Fill with 4 tablespoons of chicken mixture and 2 tablespoons of cheese. Roll up. Place in buttered 1-1/2 quart baking dish. Pour remaining sauce over tortillas. Sprinkle with the remaining cheese and reserved chilies. Bake covered at 350 degrees for 20 minutes. Cool slightly, arrange sliced mushrooms, cherry tomatoes and jalapeno peppers. Serve with salsa. Serves 4.

SENATOR PAUL D. COVERDELL - MRS. COVERDELL'S CHICKEN

Paul Coverdell

INGREDIENTS:
- 8 chicken breasts de-boned and skinless
- 1 package of bacon
- 1 package of dried beef
- 1 can of cream of mushroom soup
- 1 16 oz. container of sour cream
- 3/4 cup of milk

DIRECTIONS:
In a rectangular container spread butter on the bottom. Take the chicken breasts and roll them up and wrap a slice of bacon around each piece. Then lay them in the casserole dish.

Mix the mushroom soup, about 3/4 of the sour cream and the milk over low heat. Then cut the dried beef into small squares and put about 3/4 of this into the mixture heating.

Then pour this warm mixture over the chicken and bake at 350 degrees for about 2 hours. Sprinkle the remaining beef on the top and bake for 10 minutes.

Food Proverb
Don't count your chickens before they hatch.
What do you think this means?

GOVERNOR PETE WILSON - BARBECUE CHICKEN

My wife GAYLE and I are delighted to enclose a recipe for one of our favorite dishes. We think you will find it to be a simple and delicious way to prepare chicken.

INGREDIENTS:

4-6   chicken breasts, skinless
       Paul Newman Italian Salad Dressing
       Dijon Mustard
       Lawry's Seasoned Salt
       pepper to taste

DIRECTIONS:

First baste the chicken on all sides with mustard, then baste with salad dressing, seasoned salt and pepper. Place chicken on grill until chicken turns white on both sides. Baste once again with the same ingredients and continue grilling until meat is cooked. Enjoy!

SENATOR RICHARD SHELBY - DOVE ON THE GRILL

One of my favorite activities is hunting. This is a simple yet delicious way to prepare WILD DOVE.

2   Doves (allow at least 2 per person)
       Salt to taste
       Pepper to taste
       Worcestershire sauce to taste
1/2   slice bacon per bird

Sprinkle the dove with salt, pepper and Worcestershire sauce. Wrap each dove with bacon. Secure with toothpick if necessary. Cook over a medium fire until done, about 20 to 30 minutes. Turn occasionally.

VARIATION: Wrap 1/2 strip of bacon around a water chestnut and a boneless dove breast. Season lemon butter with Worcestershire sauce and baste frequently. Cook on grill or broil until bacon is done.

SENATOR DAVID PRYOR ORIENTAL CHICKEN SALAD

David Pryor (signature)

Due to the fact that I now try to maintain a HEALTHIER DIET, as I urge everyone to do, I am enclosing a recipe for ORIENTAL CHICKEN SALAD.

Salad:
1	large head of romaine lettuce-chopped
3	bunches watercress-chopped
1	bunch scallions-sliced
1	can water chestnuts-sliced
6 oz.	bean sprouts (fresh if possible)
3	stalks of celery-sliced

Garnish:
12	each cucumber slices
6 oz.	julienne carrot
6	each large mushrooms-sliced
6	each radish rose

Dressing:
6 oz.	olive oil
6 oz.	low sodium soy sauce
dash	of cinnamon
1	large roasting chicken breast

Preparation:
Poach or steam chicken breasts until done. (Poaching liquid can be saved for a soup or sauce). After cooling, de-bone chicken and shred using your fingers or a fork. Mix watercress, scallions, water chestnuts, bean sprouts, celery, and half of the chicken together. Toss with 1/2 of the dressing. Place romaine lettuce on plates or large bowls. Divide above mixture between bowls. Arrange two cucumber slices, 1 oz. of julienne carrot, 1 mushroom, 1 radish rose, and the rest of the chicken on top of the salad. Serve remaining dressing on the side.

GOVERNOR BRUCE KING CHICKEN ENCHILADA CASSEROLE

GOVERNOR'S MANSION CHICKEN ENCHILADA CASSEROLE

Bruce King

INGREDIENTS:

1	small can of chopped green chili
1	large can of Ashley enchilada sauce
1	can cream of chicken soup
1	small can of Pet milk
2	cups of chicken broth
1-1/2	dozen corn tortillas
2	cups of grated longhorn cheese
2	tablespoons of chopped onion
1	stewing chicken de-boned and chopped

DIRECTIONS:

Saute onions and chili in butter. Combine all liquids and add onion and chili. Break tortillas into pieces, place in casserole in layers with chicken and cheese, ending with cheese. Pour liquid over all and refrigerate overnight, or several hours. Bake at 350 degrees for one hour.

Food Proverb
A watched pot never boils.
What do you think this means?

SENATOR RICHARD G. LUGAR - SENATOR LUGAR'S FAMOUS LIME AND CILANTRO GRILLED TURKEY BREAST IN PITA POCKETS

The recipe for my Lime and Cilantro Grilled Turkey Breast in Pita Pockets is one of my family favorites. To enhance the meal, I usually serve a rice dish and spinach salad. This is an excellent meal to serve at a summer outing.

- 1-1/2 pounds of turkey breast tenderloins
- 2 limes, juiced; 1 tablespoon paprika
- 1/2 teaspoon onion salt; 1/2 teaspoon of garlic salt
- 1/2 teaspoon of cayenne pepper
- 1/4 teaspoon of white pepper
- 1/2 teaspoon of fennel seeds; 1/2 teaspoon of thyme
- 10 pitas, cut in half
- 1-1/2 cups of lettuce, shredded
- 1-1/2 cups of avocado salsa (see sauce)
- 1-1/2 cups of sour cream (see sauce)

Rub turkey with juice of limes. In a small bowl, combine paprika, onion, salt, garlic, cayenne pepper, fennel seeds and thyme. Sprinkle mixture over fillets. Cover and refrigerate for at least one hour. Preheat charcoal grill for direct heat cooking. Grill turkey 15-20 minutes until meat thermometer reaches 170 degrees Fahrenheit and turkey is no longer pink in the center. Turn turkey tenderloins over half way through grilling time. Allow turkey to stand 10 minutes. Slice into 1/4 inch strips. Fill each pita half with turkey, lettuce, avocado salsa, and if desired, the sour cream sauce. Serves 10

ANNIE LITTLE
1994 A-OK COOK-OFF
JUNIOR CHAMPION
STATE OF OKLAHOMA
ANNIE'S LITTLE
CHICKEN ROLL-UPS

1	cup cooked, chopped Tyson chicken
1/4	cup chopped onion
3/4	cup of grated Mid-America Monterey Jack cheese
2-1/4	ounce can of sliced ripe olives, well drained
1/2	cup of Aunt Harriet's Picante Sauce
1/4	teaspoon of cumin
1/4	teaspoon of pepper
4	ounce can of chopped green chilies; well drained
2	ounce jar of sliced pimentos, well drained
12	phyllo sheets
2	tablespoons Braum's butter

Heat oven to 375 degrees. Spray cookie sheet with Pam. In a large bowl, combine all ingredients except phyllo sheets and butter. Place 1 phyllo sheet on towel or large piece of waxed paper with soft edge nearest you; brush sparingly with butter. Place second sheet over the first and brush with butter; continue layering and brushing with butter on 4 additional sheets. Repeat above layering and brushing with remaining sheets to make the second stack. Spread 1/2 of chicken mixture along the short edge of each stack. Fold sides in and roll up jelly role style. Place on cookie sheet. Brush with butter. Bake at 375 degrees for 15 to 20 minutes or until golden brown. Cut each roll in half. Garnish as desired. Serves 4

GOVERNOR FIFE SYMINGTON - TURKEY SOPA

TURKEY SOPA CASSEROLE

1	doz. corn tortillas, cut into 1 inch strips
3	cups of cooked turkey or chicken
1/2	stick of butter or margarine
1	jar of Old El Paso taco sauce
1	medium onion, chopped
1	can diced green chilies
1	can cream of mushroom soup
1	can cream of chicken soup
1	can of consomme
1	lb. jack cheese, shredded
1	lb. cheddar cheese, shredded

DIRECTIONS:

Melt butter, add onions and cook until tender. Add green chilies, taco sauce, soup and turkey or chicken. Place layer of tortillas on bottom of 2 inch deep casserole. Place alternate layers of soup mixture, tortillas and cheese. Repeat for three layers making sure top layer is cheese. Bake 30 minutes at 350 degrees or until thoroughly heated and cheese is melted.
Serves 8 to 10

Using the New Food Label To Choose Healthier Foods

eed help in choosing a healthy diet? The new food label can help.

With new government regulations in force, **the new label promises to give more complete, believable and easy-to-use nutrition information than ever before.** Whether you follow a special diet or simply want to "eat healthy," you'll find the new label a helpful tool for choosing the right foods.

Eating the right foods is important because research shows that what we eat can affect our health—today and in the future. For example:
• A diet low in saturated fat and cholesterol can help reduce the risk of coronary heart disease.
• A diet rich in fruits and vegetables may help reduce the risk of some cancers.
• A diet with enough calcium is linked to a reduced risk of osteoporosis, a condition in which bones soften and become brittle.
• A diet low in sodium may help reduce the risk of high blood pressure, a risk factor for heart attack and stroke.

New information on the front, side, and even the back of food packages can help you spot foods that offer these and other healthful benefits.

What should you look for? This brochure will tell you. It describes key parts of the new label and explains how the information can help you meet your particular nutrition needs.

The New Food Label 91

The Front Label

The front label is your starting point. This is where the name of the product appears. It is here that manufacturers often place statements describing the nutritional qualities of their products. The government has set strict conditions under which these statements can be used. So when you see them, **you can believe them.**

There are two kinds of statements:

1. Nutrient Claims.

Examples include "low fat," "high fiber," "reduced calories," and "cholesterol free."

Some of these claims make a comparison to the "regular" version of the food or a similar food. For example, a *reduced-fat* claim on a jar of Italian dressing means the food has at least 25 percent less fat than regular Italian dressing. A *light* Italian dressing has at least 50 percent less fat *or* one-third fewer calories than the regular one.

Other claims show that a food is high or low in a nutrient. For example, *low-fat* Italian dressing has 3 grams of fat or less per 2-tablespoon (30-gram) serving. *Fat-free* Italian dressing has less than half a gram of fat per serving.

Examples of other claims you may see are "high fiber" on whole-wheat cereal and "low sodium" on canned green beans.

2. Health Claims.

FDA now allows claims linking a nutrient or food to the risk of a disease or health-related condition. Only health claims supported by scientific evidence are allowed.

What Can Claims Do for You?

Nutrient claims and health claims can help you quickly find foods that offer desirable nutrient levels. They can tell you if a food is low in nutrients many of us need to consume less of, such as fat, cholesterol and sodium. They also can tell you if a food is high in nutrients many of us need to consume more of, such as fiber, potassium and calcium.

For more detailed information, the claims on many products will refer you to the "Nutrition Facts," usually on the side or back of the package.

Getting All the Facts

"Nutrition Facts" is the place to go for more complete information. Here, you can easily see how a food fits into your total daily diet. Here's how to use "Nutrition Facts."

Real-Life Serving Sizes

Start with serving size information. Serving sizes are the basis for measuring a food's nutrient content. Keep in mind that serving sizes are:

- listed in both household and metric units
- uniform across product lines so that you can more easily compare the nutritional qualities of similar foods
- close to the amounts people really eat (although this doesn't mean that serving sizes are "recommended amounts").

Key
g = grams (about 28 g = 1 ounce)
mg = milligrams (1,000 mg = 1 gram)

%Daily Values—
The Key to Healthy Eating

The amounts of certain nutrients in a food are expressed in two ways:

☐ in terms of the amount by weight per serving

▪ as a percentage (%) of the Daily Value.

Nutrient amounts and %Daily Values—a new nutrition reference tool— describe the content of one serving of the food inside the packaging.

By using the %Daily Values, you can easily determine whether a food contributes a lot or a little of a particular nutrient. A high percentage means the food contains a lot of a nutrient. A low percentage means it contains a little. **You don't have to worry about doing calculations.**

But if you eat more—or less—than the serving size on the label, you'll need to adjust the amounts of nutrients accordingly. For example, the serving size for ice cream is one-half cup. If you eat one cup, you would need to double the calories and the %Daily Values listed to learn the nutritional content of the portion you eat.

The New Food Label 92

For example, let's say you're trying to eat less fat. You come across two different brands of frozen mixed vegetables in sauce. One of the packages lists 5% as the %Daily Value for total fat. The other package gives 15%. Which should you buy? The one with 5% because 5 is a significantly lower number than 15.

Keep in mind that %Daily Values are based on the amount of food usually eaten in one day. **So, the goal is to choose foods that together give you about 100% a day.** For nutrients that most of us need to eat more of—such as fiber and calcium—the goal

Let's use an example. Let's say you eat about 2,000 calories a day. Your total daily fat intake should then be no more than 65 grams. Since fat has 9 calories per gram, that amount equals 30% of your calories from fat—the upper limit recommended for most people, according to the government's Dietary Guidelines for Americans.

Let's say that the food you're preparing has 16 grams of fat per serving and shows the %Daily Value for total fat per serving at 25%. What does this tell you? It tells you that all the other foods you eat that day should total 75% *or less* of the Daily Value for total fat.

Of course, you don't have to rigidly stick to the 100% total each and every day. **Think of your diet like a budget for a vacation.** If you have $1,000 for a 10-day vacation, you can spend an average of $100 a day. If one day you want to eat at a fancy restaurant and you end up spending $150, that's okay, as long as you make up for it by spending less on other days. So it is with %Daily Values and the foods you eat. If you "splurge" on fat during a dinner of fried foods, for example, you can make up for it the next day by eating more low-fat or nonfat foods.

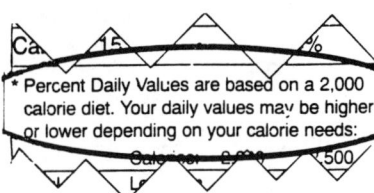

The 2,000-Calorie Basis

The nutrition panel carries a footnote explaining that the %Daily Values are based on 2,000 calories a day. Of course, not everyone eats this amount daily; some eat more, some less. Your daily calorie needs depend on many factors, such as age, height, weight, and activity level. A physician, dietitian or nutritionist can help you figure out your calorie needs.

should be to eat foods that contribute *at least* 100%. For nutrients that most of us need to eat less of—such as fat, cholesterol and sodium—the goal should be to eat *no more than* 100%.

The New Food Label 93

Whatever your daily calorie intake, you still can use the %Daily Values as a reference to help you see how a particular food fits into the context of a total daily diet.

For example, let's say you eat only 1,500 calories a day, instead of 2,000. Since 1,500 is 75% of 2,000, the %Daily Values for each of the nutrients in all the foods you eat in a day should total 75, instead of 100. So, if one food provides 25% of the Daily Value for fat, all the other foods you eat that day should add up to no more than 50%.

Ingredient Labeling— What's in a Food?

The ingredient list also can help you learn more about the foods you eat. A list of ingredients is required on almost all foods, even standardized ones like mayonnaise and bread. Ingredients are listed in descending order of weight. That helps you get an idea of the proportion of an ingredient in a food.

Also, artificial colors have to be named in the ingredient list; they no longer can be stated simply as "coloring."

And the total percentage of juice in juice drinks must be declared so that you can see exactly how much juice is in a product.

Planning a Healthier Diet

Whether you eat a regular diet or follow a special one, the new food label can serve as an important guide to better nutrition—but only if you use it.

• **Start with the front of the package.** Look for claims. You can believe them. They tell you truthfully at a glance if a food is high or low in a particular nutrient—for example, "high in fiber" or "low in fat." Claims also can help you avoid nutrients that are linked to the risk of a disease or health-related condition—for example, sodium and the risk of high blood pressure.

• **Refer to the "Nutrition Facts,"** usually on the side or back of the package, for more detailed information. Nutrition information will be on almost all processed foods. (It may also be displayed—voluntarily—at the point of purchase for many fresh fruits and vegetables and raw meat, poultry and fish). So you'll be able to learn about the nutritional qualities of almost all of the foods you buy.

• **Pay attention to the serving size.** That's what the nutrient amounts are based on. So if you eat more, or less, than the serving size listed, you need to adjust the calories and nutrient amounts accordingly.

• **Use the %Daily Values** to compare foods and see how a food fits into your total daily diet. Compare %Daily Values among similar products to help you choose the most healthful product.

• **Look at the ingredient list,** especially if you have food allergies or avoid certain ingredients for other reasons.

So, you see, it's easier than ever to know about the foods you eat. Just read the label. It can help you set a healthy table.

FROZEN MIXED VEGETABLES IN SAUCE

Nutrition Facts
Serving Size ½ cup (114g)
Servings Per Container 4

Amount Per Serving
Calories 90   Calories from Fat 30

	% Daily Value*
Total Fat 3g	5%
Saturated Fat 0g	0%
Cholesterol 0mg	0%

INGREDIENTS: Broccoli, carrots, green beans, water chestnuts, soybean oil, milk solids, modified cornstarch, salt, spices.

Rice/Eggs

HOPPIN' JOHN, PAGE 101
GRANDMA DAIGLE'S RICE DRESSING, PAGE 99
PISTACHIO RICE, PAGE 97
BAKED RICE, PAGE 97
PORK BRAINS 'N EGGS, PAGE 104

SENATOR & MRS. JOSEPH LIEBERMAN PISTACHIO RICE PILAF

Senator & Mrs. Joseph Lieberman's favorite recipe for PISTACHIO RICE PILAF

INGREDIENTS:
1/4   cup currants
2   cups of water or vegetable broth
1/2   cup of unsalted pistachio nuts
        cinnamon
1   cup of long-grain brown rice
1/4   cup of dried apricots, cut into strips

Soak currants for 15 minutes in warm water. Drain and set aside. Wash rice and drain. Place in a skillet over medium heat and stir around until it is very dry and lightly browned (be careful not to burn). Place toasted rice in a 1-1/2 quart saucepan and cover with the water or broth. Bring to a boil, reduce heat to low and cover pan with a tight-fitting lid. After the rice has simmered for about 25 minutes, place the currants, apricots and nuts on top of the rice (do not stir in). Return the lid and continue simmering 20 minutes or until rice is tender and water is absorbed. Remove from heat and let stand two minutes. Turn into a serving dish. Sprinkle cinnamon over the top.
YIELD: six servings.

CONGRESSMAN PAUL E. KANJORSKI
NALESZ NIKI (8 large crepes)

KANJORSKI FAMILY FAVORITE RECIPE
NALESZ NIKI (eight large crepes)
INGREDIENTS:
1	cup of all purpose flour
1-1/2	cups of milk
2	eggs
1	tablespoon of cooking oil
1/4	teaspoon of salt
	sugar or marmalade

Paul E. Kanjorski

DIRECTIONS:
In a bowl combine flour, milk, eggs, oil and salt. Beat well until blended and smooth. Heat a lightly greased 8 inch skillet. Remove from heat; pour 1/2 cup of batter into skillet. Lift or tilt to spread batter evenly. Return to heat; Cook on one side until lightly set. Turn with long, knife-like spatula and cook for 30 seconds longer. Sprinkle with sugar or spread with a marmalade and roll up immediately. Serve as breakfast meal.

BLUEBERRY GLAZE OPTIONAL
2-1/2	cups fresh or frozen blueberries
1/2	cup of water
3/4	cup of sugar
2	tablespoons of cornstarch
2	tablespoons of lemon juice

Combine 1 cup of blueberries with 1/2 cup of water. Bring just to boiling, reduce heat, and simmer 2 minutes. Add sugar. Combine 2 tablespoons of water and cornstarch; gradually add to blueberry mixture. Cook, stirring constantly, until thick and clear. Add 1-1/2 cups of blueberries. Cool slightly; add 2 tablespoons of lemon juice. Spoon mixture over NALESZ NIKI and roll up, topping with more blueberry mixture.

SENATOR ALFONSE D'AMATO BAKED RICE

INGREDIENTS:
- 1 cup long grain white rice
- 3 cups of boiling water
- 4 chicken bouillon cubes
- 6 tablespoons of butter
- 1 green bell pepper, chopped
- 1 clove of garlic, finely chopped
- 1/4 cup of grated cheese, romano or any hard cheese

DIRECTIONS:
Melt butter in heavy skillet and evenly brown rice. In casserole baking dish, dissolve bouillon cubes in boiling water. Stir until completely dissolved. Stir browned rice into a casserole mixture. Add cheese, bell pepper, finely chopped garlic and ground pepper to taste.
Cover and place in 350 degree oven for 30 minutes.
Yield: 4 servings
NOTE: sliced mushrooms may be added before baking.

HAROLD B. LIPSIUS KUGEL

Mr. L's KUGEL
My favorite way to serve this dish is HOT. Try it, you'll like it!

INGREDIENTS:
8	oz. fine noodles
8	oz. cream cheese
1/2	pt. sour cream
2	eggs separated (or 3)
1/4	lb. butter
2/3	cup sugar
1	teaspoon of vanilla

DIRECTIONS:
Cook noodles 10 minutes. Combine and mix all other ingredients, except egg whites, into a smooth creamy mixture.
Add noodles.
Beat egg whites with pinch of salt until soft peaks form. Fold into other ingredients.
Place in a foil lined pan 8-1/2 x 12
TOPPING - bread crumbs, sugar and cinnamon combination. Bake in 350 degree oven approximately 40 minutes or until top is browned.

Serves 6.

Food Proverb
The proof of the pudding is in the eating
What do you think this means _____

Rice/Eggs/Kugel 98

SENATOR JOHN BREAUX GRANDMA DAIGLE'S RICE DRESSING

CAJUN COOKING

I am pleased to share my favorite and my family's favorite recipes. GRANDMA DAIGLE'S RICE DRESSING, Sea food Gumbo, and Cajun deep fried Turkey. All of the enclosed recipes are from the cajun country of Louisiana where I was born. I hope everyone enjoys them as much as we do.

GRANDMA DAIGLE'S RICE DRESSING

John Breaux

INGREDIENTS:
- 1 lb. of ground meat
- 3 tablespoons of cooking oil
- 1 cup of chopped onion
- 1 cup of chopped celery
- 1 large chopped bell pepper
- 3 cups of cooked rice
- 1/2 cup of chopped green onion tops
- 1/2 cup of chopped parsley
- salt and pepper to taste
- 1 cup of water
- 2 tablespoons of Kitchen Bouquet (optional)

DIRECTIONS:
Cook meat in a large pot with the oil until brown. Add onion, celery and bell pepper. Reduce heat and cook until wilted. Add water (add more water if needed) to keep the same amount of juice that you started with. Add this to the cooked rice and keep warm until ready to serve.
Serves 10 to 12

GOVERNOR BRUCE KING QUICHE LORRAINE

GOVERNOR'S MANSION QUICHE LORRAINE

Bruce King

INGREDIENTS:
- 4 eggs
- 2 cups of cream
- 3/4 teaspoon of salt
- 1/4 teaspoon of sugar
- 1 cup of swiss cheese
- 6 slices of bacon, crispy
- 1/3 cup of onion
- 1/8 teaspoon of cayenne pepper

DIRECTIONS:
Combine eggs, cream, salt, sugar and cayenne pepper. Fry bacon crispy. Layer bacon, grated cheese and onion in bottom of pie shell. Pour in the remaining egg mixture. Bake at 425 degrees for one hour or until table knife come out clean.

PIE CRUST
- 1-3/4 cups Wondra flour
- 3/4 cup Crisco
- 1 teaspoon of salt
- ice water

Food Proverb
Don't put all your eggs in one basket.
What do you think this means _____

SENATOR MITCH McCONNELL HOPPIN' JOHN

HOPPIN' JOHN   *Mitch McConnell*

For those that are interested in quicker gratification than it takes to make BURGOO, I have included this family recipe for HOPPIN' JOHN. This is a bean and rice dish that is satisfying and easy to make. I am sure that you will find both recipes delicious.

INGREDIENTS:
- 2   cups fresh or frozen black-eyed peas
- 1/4   pound of slab bacon
- 2   small pods red peppers
- 2   cups uncooked regular rice
-       salt (to taste)

DIRECTIONS:
Cover peas with water. Simmer peas, bacon and peppers in a covered pot over low heat for 1 to 1-1/2 hours or until tender. Add rice, cover and cook over low heat, stirring frequently until rice is cooked.
Add more water during cooking if necessary. Add salt to desired taste.

Yield: 8 servings.

NEW FOOD LABEL

HOW TO READ THE

% Daily Values the KEY to HEALTHY EATING

You Can Rely on the New Label

Rest assured, when you see key words and health claims on product labels, they mean what they say as defined by the government. For example:

Key Words	What They Mean
Fat Free	Less than 0.5 gram of fat per serving
Low Fat	3 grams of fat (or less) per serving
Lean	Less than 10 grams of fat, 4 grams of saturated fat and 95 milligrams of cholesterol per serving
Light (Lite)	½ less calories or no more than ½ the fat of the higher-calorie, higher-fat version; or no more than ½ the sodium of the higher-sodium version
Cholesterol Free	Less than 2 milligrams of cholesterol and 2 grams (or less) of saturated fat per serving

To Make Health Claims About...	The Food Must Be...
Heart Disease and Fats	Low in fat, saturated fat and cholesterol
Blood Pressure and Sodium	Low in sodium
Heart Disease and Fruits, Vegetables and Grain Products	A fruit, vegetable or grain product low in fat, saturated fat and cholesterol, that contains at least 0.6 gram soluble fiber, without fortification, per serving

What's New About the Label?

It's simple. Healthy eating has never been easier, thanks to the new nutrition label. Here's the good news:

- Most foods in the grocery store must now have a nutrition label and an ingredient list.
- You can buy with confidence. Claims like "low cholesterol" and "fat free" can be used only if a food meets new legal standards set by the government.

You are looking at a new label if it's titled *Nutrition Facts*. Old labels may still be around for a while, so don't be surprised if you see them.

Why Read the Label?

Read the label to help choose foods that make up a healthful diet. Eating a healthful diet can help reduce your risk factors for some diseases. For example, too much saturated fat and cholesterol can raise blood cholesterol (a risk factor for heart disease). Too much sodium may be linked to high blood pressure. High blood pressure is a risk factor for heart attack and stroke.

No one food can make you healthy. In addition to eating healthful foods, stay active, don't smoke, and watch your weight!

How to Read the New Food Label 102

Nutrition Facts

Serving Size 1/2 cup (114g)
Servings Per Container 4

Amount Per Serving

Calories 90   Calories from Fat 30

	% Daily Value*
Total Fat 3g	5%
Saturated Fat 0g	0%
Cholesterol 0mg	0%
Sodium 300mg	13%
Total Carbohydrate 13g	4%
Dietary Fiber 3g	12%
Sugars 3g	
Protein 3g	

Vitamin A	80%	•	Vitamin C	60%
Calcium	4%	•	Iron	4%

* Percent Daily Values are based on a 2,000 calorie diet. Your daily values may be higher or lower depending on your calorie needs:

	Calories	2,000	2,500
Total Fat	Less than	65g	80g
Sat Fat	Less than	20g	25g
Cholesterol	Less than	300mg	300mg
Sodium	Less than	2,400mg	2,400mg
Total Carbohydrate		300g	375g
Fiber		25g	30g

Calories per gram:
Fat 9 • Carbohydrate 4 • Protein 4

More nutrients may be listed on some labels

Total Fat
Aim low. Most people need to cut back on fat! Too much fat may contribute to heart disease and cancer. Try to limit your calories from fat. For a healthy heart, choose foods with a big difference between the total number of calories and the number of calories from fat.

Saturated Fat
A new kind of fat? No — saturated fat is part of the total fat in food. It is listed separately because it's the key player in raising blood cholesterol and your risk of heart disease. Eat less!

Cholesterol
Too much cholesterol — a second cousin to fat — can lead to heart disease. Challenge yourself to eat less than 300 mg each day.

Sodium
You call it "salt," the label calls it "sodium." Either way, it may add up to high blood pressure in some people. So, keep your sodium intake low — 2,400 to 3,000 mg or less each day.*

*The AHA recommends no more than 3,000 mg sodium per day for healthy adults.

Daily Value
Feel like you're drowning in numbers? Let the Daily Value be your guide. Daily Values are listed for people who eat 2,000 or 2,500 calories each day. If you eat more, your personal daily value may be higher than what's listed on the label. If you eat less, your personal daily value may be lower.

For fat, saturated fat, cholesterol and sodium, choose foods with a low % Daily Value. For total carbohydrate, dietary fiber, vitamins and minerals, your daily value goal is to reach 100% of each.

g = grams (About 28 g = 1 ounce)
mg = milligrams (1,000 mg = 1 g)

Serving Size
Is your serving the same size as the one on the label? If you eat double the serving size listed, you need to double the nutrient and calorie values. If you eat one-half the serving size shown here, cut the nutrient and calorie values in half.

Calories
Are you overweight? Cut back a little on calories! Look here to see how a serving of the food adds to your daily total. A 5' 4", 138-lb. active woman needs about 2,200 calories each day. A 5' 10", 174-lb. active man needs about 2,900. How about you?

Total Carbohydrate
When you cut down on fat, you can eat more carbohydrates. Carbohydrates are in foods like bread, potatoes, fruits and vegetables. Choose these often! They give you more nutrients than sugars like soda pop and candy.

Dietary Fiber
Grandmother called it "roughage," but her advice to eat more is still up-to-date! That goes for both soluble and insoluble kinds of dietary fiber. Fruits, vegetables, whole-grain foods, beans and peas are all good sources and can help reduce the risk of heart disease and cancer.

Protein
Most Americans get more protein than they need. Where there is animal protein, there is also fat and cholesterol. Eat small servings of lean meat, fish and poultry. Use skim or low-fat milk, yogurt and cheese. Try vegetable proteins like beans, grains and cereals.

Vitamins & Minerals
Your goal here is 100% of each for the day. Don't count on one food to do it all. Let a combination of foods add up to a winning score.

How to Read the New Food Label 103

CONGRESSMAN HOWARD COBLE PORK BRAINS 'N EGGS A SOUTHERN DELIGHT

Below is a recipe of my favorite breakfast, BRAINS 'N EGGS. As a youngster my MOM used to prepare Brains 'n Eggs for our breakfast. It was a fairly regular breakfast in our house and not at all unusual. That's when I started eating them. I have enjoyed them ever since, but I can't find any on CAPITOL HILL. I'll admit the name of the dish is not the most appetizing name, but try'em, you might like'em.

PORK BRAINS 'N EGGS ... A SOUTHERN DELIGHT

INGREDIENTS:
- 2-1/2 tablespoons of bacon grease
- 4 eggs
- 1/3 cup of whole milk
- 1/4 teaspoon of fresh ground black pepper
- 1/4 teaspoon salt
- 1 can (5 oz.) pork brains packed in gravy (Rose brand preferred)

DIRECTIONS:
Melt bacon grease in iron skillet on low heat. Add pork brains to heated grease and stir with a fork, and add the salt and pepper. Whisk eggs and milk together, increase heat, add egg mixture to brains. Scramble to desired consistency and immediately serve over toast. For a truly SOUTHERN DISH, serve with grits and apple butter. Serves 2

Salads

APPLE SALAD, PAGE 106
AMBROSIA FRUIT &NUT MOLD, PAGE 107
POTATO SALAD, PAGE 106
SPINACH SALAD, PAGE 108
TOMATO & ONION SALAD, PAGE 108
VEGETABLE SALAD, PAGE 105

SENATOR SAM NUNN VEGETABLE SALAD

1	can of white corn
1	can cut green beans
1	can of English peas
1	can La Choy fancy Chinese vegetables
1-1/2	cups of chopped celery
1	medium sweet onion, chopped
1	small package of slivered almonds, toasted
1/3	cup of sugar
1/4	cup dark vinegar
1/2	cup of salad oil
1	teaspoon of salt
1	teaspoon of pepper

Drain canned vegetables and mix with celery, onion and almonds.
Mix last five ingredients together and pour over vegetables. Marinate for several hours.

JOE FIORENTINO APPLE/WALNUT SALAD

Joe Fiorentino

10	red apples
5	stalks of celery, finely diced
	sugar pinch
1	cup of walnuts, broken into small pieces
1/2	cup of mayonnaise

Wash, pare, quarter, core and dice red apples. Place into a large bowl. Add walnuts, celery, mayonnaise, sugar, salt and pepper. Mix well, refrigerate before serving.

POTATO SALAD

15	potatoes, large (approx. 5 lbs.)
5	stalks of celery, finely chopped (2 cups) pare to remove veins
2	onions, medium, finely chopped
1	tablespoon of fresh parsley, finely chopped
1	tablespoon of vinegar
1	teaspoon of celery seed
1	carrot, finely chopped
1	small dill pickle, finely chopped
1/2	cup of mayonnaise
	salt and pepper, to taste

Wash and boil potatoes until tender and test with fork. Remove potato skin and section into 1/2 inch cubes. Combine all the above ingredients and mix well. Cover and refrigerate before serving.
Serves 8 to 10

GOVERNOR E. BENJAMIN NELSON - AMBROSIA FRUIT AND NUT MOLD

AMBROSIA FRUIT AND NUT MOLD

INGREDIENTS:
- 2   3 oz. packages of lime jello
- 2-1/2   cups of boiling water
- 1   small jar of maraschino cherries, chopped
- 1   small can of crushed pineapple, undrained
- 1   pint sour cream
- 1/2   cup of walnuts

DIRECTIONS:
Dissolve Jello in water. Set aside; when thoroughly cooled, add sour cream and mix well with mixer, on slowest speed. Fold in the rest of ingredients. Pour into greased mold and refrigerate for one hour. When ready to serve, place mold in pan of warm water briefly to loosen and then turn into serving dish.

Salad

JOE FIORENTINO SPINACH SALAD

1	pound fresh spinach, wash and remove stems
1	pound mushrooms, washed and sliced
2	tomatoes, cut to wedge
1/2	green pepper, cut to rings
1/2	red pepper, cut to rings
6	green onions
1	onion, cut to rings
12	black olives
	dash garlic powder, salt, black pepper

Wash and remove stems from spinach. Slice mushrooms, tomatoes, green peppers, red peppers, green onions and onion. Combine all ingredients above in a large bowl, add dash of garlic powder. Mix and cover. Refrigerate for 1 hour before serving. Salt and pepper to taste, serve lemon wedge with each portion or use your favorite salad dressing.

TOMATO & ONION SALAD

3 large tomatoes, sliced
1 large onion, sliced
  oregano (pinch)
3 teaspoons of olive oil
  salt to taste
  pepper to taste
  garlic powder (dash)

Mix all ingredients well. In a flat dish arrange onion rings under and over the tomatoes. Season to taste. Cover and refrigerate one hour before serving.

PAUL JAY FINK, M.D. ASSOCIATE VICE PRESIDENT, ALBERT EINSTEIN HEALTHCARE FOUNDATION

THE DIRECTOR OF EINSTEIN CENTER FOR THE STUDY OF VIOLENCE.

PARENTING RECIPE for the DEVELOPMENT of A CARING NON-VIOLENT ADULT

1. The child is helpless and needs 100 percent love and attention during the first year of life.
2. The child begins to search his/her environment in the second year of life and this curiosity is insatiable - don't find reason to flex your muscles with someone who is unable to understand what you want.
3. The child seeks to control his/her world in the third year of life - both the inner world: bowels, bladder, speech, thought, and action, and the outer world: loved ones, objects, pets, anything animate or inanimate.
4. The small child is not malicious, ornery, spiteful or an adult. If you adultify the child you cause enormous confusion.
5. Children are small and helpless - hitting them does no good and while it may help them to control their behavior, it also teaches them to hate the people upon whom they depend.
6. Children learn to obey and produce best when they feel loved, when they are made to feel proud of what they do, and when they are guided with warmth and joy.
7. Children learn rapidly and need to be guided and instructed in ways that make learning a pleasure which sets the tone for life.

If parents can do these things for the first 10 years of their child's life and then get through the second 10 years with both themselves and the child alive, the result should be a beautiful, loving, empathic, and caring adult.

Parenting Recipe 109

delicious MENU

JANUARY
SUPER BOWL SUNDAY BUFFET
We kick off the day with the T.V. set on and at full blast. While the pre-game show is on, the drinks are served: Bloody Marys, beer and soda. The table is set and the buffet includes shrimp cocktail with shrimp dip (see sauce/dips) potato chips and pretzels bowls, Pasta Lasagna (see Pasta), fresh salad bowl (see salad), garlic bread, rolls (see bread), chocolate cheese cake (see cakes) soft molasses cookies (see cakes/cookies). Georgia Pecan Pie (see Pies) and plenty of hot coffee.

MARCH
VICKI GUITERAS GIUNTA......
St. Patrick's Day... A Paddy Party

HOLIDAY FAVORITES

St. Patrick's Day comes during a long stretch of social inactivity, between the holidays of New Year's and Easter. This has always been a welcome reason for a party. I start off with a lot of green and white decorations and cheerful Irish music.
MENU: Fresh cut raw vegetables, as hors d'oeuvres with salsa and yogurt dips. Corned beef and cabbage, baked potatoes, to be washed down with plenty of cold beer. Bowls of green jello and Irish sweet potato candy for dessert.

APRIL
CATHY McGRAW ......Easter Sunday Dinner
My husband John and I have been hosting the Easter Sunday Dinner for the last 16 years. My family keeps coming back every year, and every year I get "RAVE REVIEWS" The
APPETIZERS- Mushroom Bread, and cheese cocktail swirl.
MAIN COURSE- Baked Ham with Pineapples, Fresh steamed Asparagus, candied baby carrots, pineapple filling and scalloped potatoes.
Rolls and butter, and for DESSERT my children Lauren, Cate and Jeff enjoy the Bunny Rabbit cake and vanilla ice cream.

Passover, the first of the major Jewish festivals mentioned in the Bible, is observed and celebrated by more Jewish people than any other holiday in the Jewish calendar.

The basic concept of Passover is freedom, in every connotation. Historically, Passover celebrates the escape of the Israelites from Egyptian bondage. We can also reflect on present times and be thankful for the good that surrounds us each day.

The Passover Seder (dinner) is the gathering of family and friends for the purpose of remembering the Israelites plight under Egyptian rule and the eventual celebration of freedom. Traditionally, this story is read by family members from a Haggadah. I will always have wonderful memories of seeing my extended family together. There was always alot laughing and reminiscing. The children were always running around having a great time. When all the food was prepared, we sat down to a spectacular feast. On the dinner table we placed the Seder Plate, which holds the foods symbolic of life under Egyptian rule.

1. Charoses - a mixture of chopped nuts, apples, wine, and cinnamon, is reminiscent of the mortar used by the Israelites in building cities for the Egyptians. The pleasant taste symbolizes many things, including God's kindness to us.

2. Roasted Shankbone - This bone is symbolic of the sacrifice of the paschal lamb on the eve of the departure from Egypt. A roasted chicken neck can also be used.

3. Roasted Egg - represents the regular festival sacrifice brought in the days when the Temple stood in Jerusalem. In addition, the egg symbolizes rebirth we experience each spring.

4. Karpas - watercress or parsley to remind us of the meagerness of life in Egypt and also the greeness of the Spring season.

5. Maror - most often served in the form of horseradish, symbolizes the bitterness of slavery.

6. Matzos - unleavened bread represents our ancestors' hasty exodus from Egypt. "They picked up their dough before it had time to leaven."

Traditional Passover Menu

Passover Wines
Matzhos
Matzoh Ball Soup
Gefilte Fish w/Horseradish
Brisket of Beef
Roast Chicken
Matzoh Charlotte (kugel)
Tzimmes (honeyed carrot preparation)
Fresh Fruits
Desserts prepared specially for the Passover holiday
Coffee, Tea

Gary E. Hendler is the President of Suburban Real Estate Rentals & Sales, Inc. which is located outside of Philadelphia, Pennsylvania. His company specializes in residential rentals and management targeted to an upscale clientel.

Steaks

Sirloin Steak (8 oz)
Prime sirloin, grilled as you like it, served with baked potato **$8.95**

Beef Medallions
An 8 oz filet sliced and grilled to your order is served with rice ... **$9.95**

Prime Prime Rib
The King's Cut ... **$12.95**
The Queen's Cut... **$8.95**
Horseradish or au jus.

Filet Mignon
Choice 8 oz cut marinated to tasty perfection and wrapped in bacon.. **$8.50**

Chopped Sirloin (½ lb)
Grilled to order over an open flame and seasoned with special spices.. **$8.95**

JULY
JOE FIORENTINO JR.

4TH OF JULY BARBECUE. What a great time of the year to have a barbecue. Eating food outside in the sun and the fresh air is very enjoyable especially with the wonderful smell of food that is cooking on the grill. When my father asked me to give him a menu for his cookbook, I chose the 4th of July barbecue because it's a fun day that starts with a parade and ends with fireworks, all day long the grill cooks up plenty of spare ribs, hot dogs, hamburgers, fried chicken, hot and sweet sausage and corn on the cob wrapped in aluminum foil. On the table is a large pot of baked beans, next to trays of lettuce and tomatoes, sliced onion, potato salad, pickles, olives, potato chips, pretzels, marshmallows and plenty of draft beer from the keg. Oh yes, Apple Pie is a must on the 4th of July, or is it said, the 4th of July and Apple Pie.

I am the pit boss most of the day, not the Casino kind, but the back yard kind.

NOVEMBER
THANKSGIVING DAY DINNER

This is the day we give thanks and eat too much turkey. We start with tomato juice, a 25 pound roasted turkey (see how to cook a perfect turkey), bread stuffing, cranberry sauce, French-cut string beans (see vegetables), potato / walnut salad (see salad), vegetable salad (see vegetables), mashed potatoes, rolls & cranberry bread (see bread) Georgia pecan pie (see pie), Yum Yum cake (see cake) coffee, tea and Wassail (see beverages) and the Fiorentino traditional- figs stuffed with walnuts (see December menu)

DECEMBER

GLORIA F. MOPPERT......CHRISTMAS DINNER. has always been very special to my husband Bill and myself. It is a happy and joyous day with the gathering of all our children, their spouses and our grandchildern. Before dinner we serve cocktails, red or white wine and assortment of hors d oeuvres. We start dinner with a prayer of thanks said by one of my children. This year it will be Harry, last year it was Billy, next year it will be Stevie and then Vicki will start the rotation all over again.

CHICKEN SOUP with Escarole (sometimes called Wedding soup). It is delicious and is made with one whole chicken, carrots, celery, parsley and cooked escarole. Just before serving mix one beaten egg and grated Italian cheese on top of soup while cooking.

TURKEY (28 lbs.) stuffed with filling. Mashed potatoes, sweet potatoes, fresh string beans, fresh broccoli, fresh carrots, mushrooms (sliced and cooked in tomato sauce).

SALAD lettuce, tomatoes, onions, black olives, croutons, celery sticks, green olives. Hot dinner rolls, cranberry sauce, coffee and tea.

DESSERT Yum Yum cake (see cake) apple, cherry, coconut pies, dinner mints and another family tradition-(FIGS and NUTS), walnuts stuffed inside the fig like a small sandwich.

HOLIDAY MENU

DECEMBER

KWANZAA is a holiday based on the rich African heritage. Kwanzaa is celebrated from December 26th to January 1st. During this time the Seven principles are observed that will benefit the family and the community.

NGUZO SABA (The Seven Principles)
1. UMOJA (Unity)
2. KUJICHAGULIA (Self-determination)
3. UJIMA (Collective Work and Responsibility)
4. UJAMAA (Cooperative Economics)
5. NIA (Purpose)
6. KUUMBA (Creativity)
7. IMANI (Faith)

THE FAMOUS PEOPLE COOKBOOK

BEVERAGES
PASTA
VEGETABLES
SANDWICHES
MEAT
eat
BREAD
Buffet
Cake
Southern Fried
delicious
Chocolate
Appetizers
MENU
POULTRY
EATS
SALAD
What's Cookin' in the U. S. A.
CAKES
COOKIES
BRUNCH
Seafood
From The Grill
CAJUN
COOKING
Soup
eat
PIES
RICE
DIPS
SAUCE
STEAKS
NOODLES
EGGS

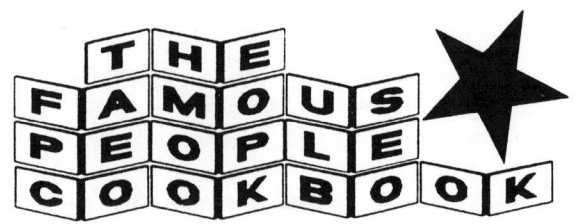

Sauce/Dips

AVOCADO SALAD, PAGE 118
CAJUN SAUCE FOR DIPPING, PAGE 117
CHIP DIP, PAGE 117
GARBANZO DIP, PAGE 118
PAPRIKA SAUCE, PAGE 116
SHRIMP DIP, PAGE 115
SOUR CREAM SAUCE, PAGE 116

SENATOR DAVE DURENBERGER SHRIMP DIP

2	4-1/2 oz. cans of shrimp
1	8 oz. package of cream cheese
1/4	pound, melted butter
2	tablespoons of lemon juice
dash	Worcestershire sauce
to taste	grated onions
1/4	cup of mayonnaise

Blend ingredients together and refrigerate overnight. Serve on crackers.

This recipe will keep for long periods of time when refrigerated.

SENATOR JOHN D. ROCKEFELLER IV PAPRIKA SAUCE

- 3 tablespoons of butter
- 3 medium tomatoes
- 3 tablespoons of onion, finely chopped
- 2 tablespoons of sour cream
- 1/4 cup of all purpose flour
- 1 tablespoon paprika
- salt and pepper to taste

Peel tomatoes and coarsely chop. You should have approximately 3-1/2 cups.
Finely chop the onions for three tablespoons. Melt two tablespoons of butter in a skillet. Add the onion and simmer until transparent and soft, do not brown. Stir in the flour and paprika, then stir in the tomatoes and add salt and pepper. Simmer fifteen minutes, stirring frequently. Stir in the sour cream. Swirl in the remaining butter by rotating the pan gently. Taste and correct with salt and pepper. Serve hot.

SENATOR RICHARD G. LUGAR - SOUR CREAM SAUCE

- 1 cup sour cream
- 1 teaspoon of salt
- 1/4 cup of green onions, minced
- 1/4 cup of green chilies, minced
- 1/4 teaspoon cayenne pepper
- 1/2 teaspoon of black pepper

In a small bowl, combine ingredients, cover and refrigerate until ready to use.

GOVERNOR E. BENJAMIN NELSON - CHIP DIP

1 can shrimp, drained and rinsed
1/2 cup of chili sauce
8 oz. cream cheese, softened
1/2 cup of mayonnaise
1/4 cup chopped onion
2 teaspoons of horseradish

Blend chili sauce into cream cheese. Mix in rest of ingredients. Add shrimp carefully. Chill and serve.

GOVERNOR MIKE LOWRY - CAJUN SAUCE FOR DIPPING

2 cups of olive oil
1/2 cup of wine vinegar
4 tablespoons of creole mustard
1 teaspoon of horseradish
1 teaspoon of paprika
1 tablespoon of salt
1 tablespoon of pepper
1/4 cup of celery, chopped
3 green onions, chopped
1/4 cup of parsley, chopped

Combine vinegar with mustard, horseradish, paprika, salt and pepper. Gradually add olive oil while whipping vigorously. Add remaining finely minced ingredients.

CAJUN COOKING

Sauce/Dips 117

SENATOR SAM NUNN GARBANZO DIP

The peach bread is very tasty and for the people that are a little health conscious, I have enclosed a recipe for Garbanzo bean dip, red snapper and a vegetable salad.

GARBANZO DIP
1   pound 4 ounce can Garbanzo beans
1   tablespoon of olive oil
1/2 teaspoon of sesame seeds
    freshly ground pepper (to taste)
1   large clove of garlic, minced
3   tablespoons of lemon juice

Drain the chickpeas and combine all the ingredients in the blender until creamy. Serve chilled and sprinkle with fresh chopped parsley.

Healthful as a dip for raw vegetables or as a spread with pita bread. Thirty-five calories per serving (1 tablespoon).

SENATOR RICHARD G. LUGAR - AVOCADO SALSA

Dick Lugar

AVOCADO SALSA
1   avocado, diced
1   lime, juiced
2   tomatoes, seeded and diced
1/2 cup green onion, minced
1/2 cup green pepper minced
1/2 cup fresh cilantro

In a small bowl, combine avocado and lime juice. Stir in remaining ingredients. Cover and refrigerate before use.

Seafood

NORFOLK CRAB CAKES, PAGE 128
CRABMEAT SUPREME, PAGE 121
STEAMED BLUE CRABS, PAGE 123
FISH FILLETS IN SOUR CREAM, PAGE 130
HALIBUT PARMESAN, PAGE 122
SWEET & SOUR HALIBUT, PAGE 125
SOUTH OF THE BORDER KATFISH, PAGE 126
OYSTER CASSEROLE, PAGE 131
RED SNAPPER, PAGE 119
SALMONBURGERS, PAGE 122
SEAFOOD GUMBO, PAGE 124
BAKED SHAD & ROE, PAGE 121
BARBECUE SHRIMP, PAGE 129
FILLET OF SOLE, PAGE 120

SENATOR SAM NUNN RED SNAPPER

RED SNAPPER

1/2	cup minced onion
3	tablespoons fresh orange juice
2	tablespoons oil
2	teaspoons grated orange peel
1/2	teaspoon salt
	Dash nutmeg and ground pepper
4	snapper fillets

Combine onion, oil, orange juice, and peel, and salt in greased (12x8x2) pan. Arrange snapper fillets in this mixture, turning to coat evenly. Let stand at room temperature for 30 minutes (lightly cover dish). Add nutmeg and pepper. Bake at 400 degrees for about 12 minutes or until fillets flake easily. Baste and serve immediately.

CONGRESSMAN WILLIAM H. ZELIFF JR.
FILLET OF SOLE IN BUTTER, LEMON AND WINE

Sydna Zeliff

Recipe from Bill and Sydna Zeliff

INGREDIENTS:
1/4	cup of butter
1	tablespoon of flour
2	tablespoons of lemon juice
1	tablespoon of snipped parsley
	dash salt and pepper
1/4	teaspoon of celery seed
1/4	cup of white wine
1	lb. of fresh sole fillet

DIRECTIONS:
Place butter in pie plate. Microwave on high until melted. Blend in the remaining ingredients except fish fillets. Coat both sides of fish with sauce. Arrange in pie plate and cover with waxed paper. Microwave on high about 6 to 8 minutes or until fish flakes easily in the center with a fork. Serve with slices of tomato on top of the fish.
Serves 4
This recipe is a variation of one from the Sharp Microwave Book

Food Proverb
After the feast comes the reckoning
What do you think this means _____

SENATOR CONNIE MACK MRS. PRISCILLA MACK'S FAVORITE RECIPE FOR CRABMEAT SUPREME

8	slices of bread (white) cubed
2	cups of crabmeat (fresh claw)
1	yellow onion
1/2	cup of mayo
1	cup of celery
1/2	cup of green peppers, chopped
4	beaten eggs
1	cup of mushroom soup (can)
	dash paprika
3	cups of milk

Cook celery in water boiling for 10 minutes. Put 4 cut pieces of bread in bottom of pan. Mix crab, onion, mayo, pepper and celery and spread over bread. Place 4 pieces of bread on top. Mix egg and milk. Pour over all. Cover and place in refrigerator for 1 hour or more. Bake 15 minutes at 325 degrees in 9-1/2x13 inch pan. Spoon soup over the top, sprinkle with paprika or cheese or both. Bake for 1 hour. Serves 4

SENATOR WILLIAM V. ROTH JR. BAKED SHAD AND ROE

1	medium to large shad, split
1	set shad roe
1/2	pint sour cream
	paprika
	lemon slices

Place the fish in a shallow baking dish, with the skin side down. Lay a piece of roe on each piece of fish. Cover the fish and roe with a thick layer of sour cream. Sprinkle with paprika. Put two thin lemon slices on each piece of fish. Bake 30 minutes at 400 degrees.

GOVERNOR WALTER J. HICKEL SALMONBURGERS

A FAVORITE AT THE GOVERNOR HOUSE IN JUNEAU, ALASKA

INGREDIENTS:

1	pound cooked salmon, fresh or canned
2	medium size raw potatoes, grated
2	eggs
1	medium onion, minced
	seasoning, to taste

DIRECTIONS:
Combine all ingredients working into a soft batter. Make patty salmonburgers and fry them as you would a hamburger. Allow sufficient time to cook the potato.

PARMESAN HALIBUT

A FAVORITE AT THE GOVERNOR'S HOUSE IN JUNEAU, ALASKA

PARMESAN HALIBUT

1/3	cup grated parmesan
3	tablespoons of four
1-1/2	lbs. of halibut steaks or fillets
3	tablespoons of butter or margarine
2	tablespoons of parsley, chopped

Combine the cheese and flour. Cut halibut into serving size portions and dip into the mixture. Saute in butter until fish flakes when tested with a fork. Remove from pan and place on platter. Pour the drippings over the fish and sprinkle with parsley. Serves 4.

GOVERNOR WILLIAM DONALD SCHAEFER
Steamed Blue Crabs the "Truly Maryland Way"
Maryland Blue Crabs

Since it is an honor to be the Governor of the great State of Maryland, naturally, my favorite food is seafood-particularly when it is fresh from our Chesapeake Bay. It is my pleasure to enclose as requested, a recipe for one of Maryland's Best seafood dishes-Steamed Crabs. How to open Maryland Steamed Crabs. STEAMED BLUE CRABS THE "TRULY MARYLAND WAY".

- 1/2 cup seafood seasoning
- 1/2 cup of salt
- 3 cups of white vinegar
- 3 cups of beer (or water)
- 3 dozen live Maryland Blue hard Crabs

Mix seasonings, vinegar and beer (or water), well. Put one-half of the crabs in a large pot with a rack and tight fitting lid. Pour one-half the seasonings over the top. Add rest of crabs and remaining liquid. Steam covered until crabs turn bright red in color, about 20 to 30 minutes. Serve hot or cold.

Makes about 9 to 12 servings, depending on size of crabs.

NOTE: Serve crabs immediately if to be eaten hot. To serve cold bring to room temperature and refrigerate until ready to use. Under NO CIRCUMSTANCES should live and steamed crabs ever be stored in such a manner that they could come into contact with each other.

HOW TO OPEN MARYLAND STEAMED CRABS

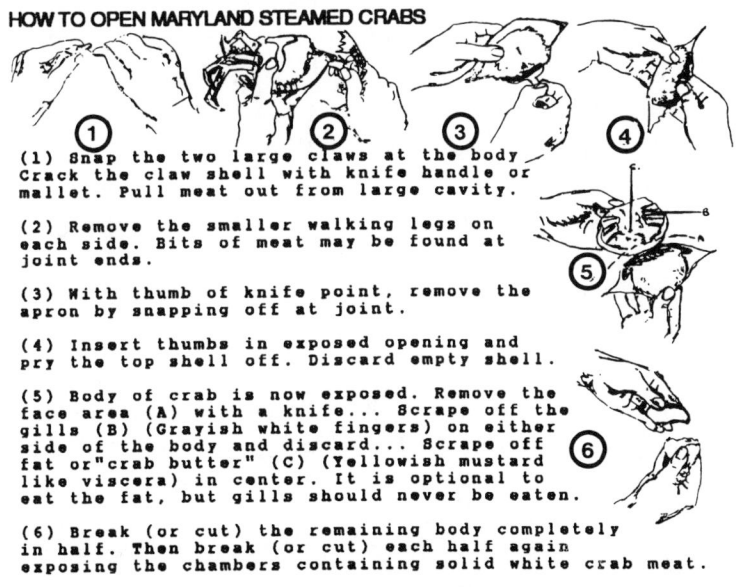

(1) Snap the two large claws at the body. Crack the claw shell with knife handle or mallet. Pull meat out from large cavity.

(2) Remove the smaller walking legs on each side. Bits of meat may be found at joint ends.

(3) With thumb of knife point, remove the apron by snapping off at joint.

(4) Insert thumbs in exposed opening and pry the top shell off. Discard empty shell.

(5) Body of crab is now exposed. Remove the face area (A) with a knife... Scrape off the gills (B) (Grayish white fingers) on either side of the body and discard... Scrape off fat or "crab butter" (C) (Yellowish mustard like viscera) in center. It is optional to eat the fat, but gills should never be eaten.

(6) Break (or cut) the remaining body completely in half. Then break (or cut) each half again exposing the chambers containing solid white crab meat.

SENATOR JOHN BREAUX
SEAFOOD GUMBO CAJUN COOKING

I am pleased to share my favorite and my family's favorite recipes. SEAFOOD GUMBO, CAJUN DEEP FRIED TURKEY, AND GRANDMA DANGLE'S RICE DRESSING. All the enclosed recipes are from the Cajun country of Louisiana where I was born. I hope everyone enjoys them as much as we do.

John Breaux

SEAFOOD GUMBO
INGREDIENTS:
- 1 cup of flour
- 1 cup cooking oil
- 2 cups of onion, chopped
- 1/2 cup of green onion tops, chopped
- 1/4 cup of parsley, chopped
- 2-1/2 quarts of hot water
- 1 tablespoon of salt
- 1 teaspoon of cayenne or red pepper
- 1 lb. crabmeat or 2 cans of crabmeat
- 2 lbs of shrimp, raw and peeled
- 1 pint of oysters with liquid

DIRECTIONS:
ROUX: Mix flour and oil together in a 4 cup measure. Microwave on high 7 minutes. Stir well, microwave on high for 30 SECONDS more. Roux will be dark caramel.

GUMBO: In large cooking pot, add hot water, roux, onion, green onion tops, parsley, salt and pepper. Cover and cook on high 15 minutes. Add crabmeat, and cook on high for 15 minutes more. Add shrimp and oysters and cook on MEDIUM for 20 minutes. Serve as a soup with rice

GOVERNOR WALTER J. HICKEL SWEET AND SOUR HALIBUT

A FAVORITE AT THE GOVERNOR'S HOUSE IN JUNEAU, ALASKA
SWEET AND SOUR HALIBUT

2	lbs. of halibut
	salted water enough to cover fish
1/2	dry onion, chopped
1	slice of lemon
1	sprig of parley, chopped
	several peppercorns
1	clove of garlic, minced
1/2	cup of pineapple juice
1/2	cup of water
4	teaspoons of cornstarch
2	tablespoons of brown sugar
1/4	cup of cider vinegar
1	tablespoon of soy sauce
8	oz. drained pineapple chunks
1/2	green pepper, chunked
3	green onions, sliced
2	tablespoons of sherry

DIRECTIONS:
Place halibut in simmering salted water seasoned with onion, lemon, parsley peppercorn and garlic. Cover and simmer 5 to 7 minutes or until halibut flakes when tested with fork. Drain.

With the one cup of pineapple juice and water, combine cornstarch, brown sugar, vinegar and soy sauce. Cook, stirring constantly, until thick and clear.

Add pineapple chunks, green pepper chunks, green onion slices, and sherry. Cook one minute longer.

Pour over poached halibut. Serve and enjoy.

JANNIKA PERCELL 1994 A-OK COOK-OFF SENIOR CHAMPION STATE OF OKLAHOMA SOUTH of the BORDER KATFISH

SPANISH RICE
1   (10-3/4 ounce) can chicken broth
1   tablespoon of Bake-Rite vegetable oil
1   cup of long grain rice (uncooked)
1   medium tomato (peeled, seeded and chopped)
1   clove of garlic (crushed)
2   Padre jalapeno peppers (seeded and minced)
1/2   teaspoon ground cumin

FISH
4   (6 ounce) Aquafarms catfish fillets
2   teaspoons of peanut oil
1/4   teaspoon of Griffith's ground pepper
1/4   teaspoon of cayenne pepper

DRESSING
1/4   cup of peanut oil
1/2   teaspoon of DOX chili seasoning
1/4   teaspoon of salt
2   cloves of garlic (crushed)
1/4   cup lime juice

SPANISH RICE Heat oil in large skillet. Add rice, cook, stirring constantly until a golden brown. Stir in broth and next 4 ingredients; bring mixture to a boil. Cover, reduce heat, and simmer 25 to 30 minutes or until liquid is absorbed.

DRESSING Combine all ingredients in a sauce pan; cook over medium heat until thoroughly heated, stirring constantly. Serve warm. Yield 1/2 cup.

FISH Arrange fillets in a shallow pan, combine peanut oil, ground pepper and cayenne pepper; brush over fish. Broil 6 inches from heat for 8 to 10 minutes or until fish flakes easily when tested with a fork. Place fillets on Spanish rice and drizzle with dressing. Serve immediately. Yield 4 servings.

GOVERNOR MIKE LOWRY SHRIMP BOWL RECIPE

60-70	thawed shrimp (25-30 count) per pound
2	gallons of water
12	bay leaves
1	teaspoon of mustard seed
1/2	teaspoon of basil
1/4	teaspoon of whole cloves
1	teaspoon of red pepper
	pinch of celery seed, fennel seed, caraway seed, peppercorns, cumin seed
1/8	teaspoon of ground marjoram
1/8	teaspoon of thyme leaves
1	small dry onion
2	stalks of celery
3	cloves of garlic
1/2	lemon
2	tablespoons of sea salt
4	teaspoons of cayenne pepper
3	tablespoons of Worcestershire sauce
1	cup of white wine

Heat water to boiling. Add the seasonings and coarsely chopped fruits and vegetables. Cook for 30 minutes. Add shrimp and cook 5 minutes more. Serve with Cajun Sauce.

CAJUN SAUCE for Dipping

2	cups of olive oil
1/2	cup of wine vinegar
4	tablespoons of creole mustard
1	teaspoon of horseradish
1	teaspoon of paprika
1	tablespoon of salt
1	tablespoon of pepper
1/4	cup of chopped celery
3	chopped green onions
1/4	cup of chopped parsley

Combine vinegar with mustard, horseradish, paprika, salt and pepper. Gradually add olive oil while whipping vigorously. Add remaining finely minced ingredients.

SENATOR JOHN WARNER
NORFOLK CRAB CAKES

John Warner

CHEF'S NOTE: This is a creative recipe and precise measurments, preparation of the mix, and cooking variables are trade secrets known only to the chef! Traditional crab cakes are those made with a mix of the ingredients recomended below and the amounts to suit the chef's particular taste.

Fresh Chesapeake Bay blue crab meat (crabs from the Virginia side) Fresh onions, preferably at least two types for variety of flavor and texture, green bell peppers, parsley, pepper, bread crumbs,(or a mix with corn bread),heavy cream,eggs,butter.

(1) Pre-cook onions, don't lose firmness.

(2) Slightly sautee chopped green bell peppers to release full flavor. Note:-Pre-cooking onions, peppers, cornmeal,(if used), at the end of this step reduces amount of cooking to which the crabmeat is subjected. You can purchase crabmeat packaged and fully cooked, but any further heat diminishes quality. Don't make this common mistake.

(3) Mix crabmeat, egg, cooked onions, green peppers, bread crumbs, and black pepper. Note- Another mistake is adding salt. Crabmeat contains the delicate flavor of "sea salt", don't try to improve on nature ! If the "eaters" want to add salt, let them "eat cake" instead !

(4) Add sufficient cream to bind the mixture lightly.

(5) Now you are ready to cook the mixture, first let's pre-cook the butter. It might suprise you to learn that butter tastes better,is more digestible, and browns the outside of the cake quicker if heated slowly. When you see a light browning of the solids from the butter in the pan quickly add the hand molded crab cake, before butter begins to burn. This takes skillful timing and, once mastered, elevates you to CHEF!

(6) Cooking. If you have done a proper job of pre-cooking ingredients (less crabmeat), allowing this mixture to achieve room temperature,preparing the butter, the rest is easy. Add crab cake, no more than 1/2-3/4 inches thick. A thicker crab cake will tend to overcook on the outside, while not cooking the inside properly. Got it?

(7) By now you have had enough of this recipe- especially the advice. Two last hints. The less you have to cook the crab cake,the better which preserves the seasoning of the sea, one of natures finest gifts. When done, remove from pan, don't let it soak up excess butter.

(8) Good luck, and thank you for joining me in this venture.

GOVERNOR CARROLL A. CAMPBELL, JR. BARBECUE SHRIMP

BARBECUE SHRIMP

INGREDIENTS:
Marinating Sauce:
- 1/4 cup olive oil
- 3 tablespoons lemon juice
- 1/4 cup of Italian dressing
- 2 lbs. of shrimp

Barbecue Sauce:
- 3 tablespoons of catsup
- 2 tablespoons of white vinegar
- 1 tablespoon of Worcestershire sauce
- 4 tablespoons of water
- 2 tablespoons of oil
- 3 tablespoons of sugar
- 1 teaspoon of mustard
- 1 teaspoon of chili powder
- 1/2 teaspoon of pepper

Directions:
Boil shrimp in salted water. Cool, clean and peel. Put shrimp in marinating sauce and chill for 1 hour. Drain off marinating sauce and cover with barbecue sauce. Mix well. Let sit in refrigerator for 1 hour or longer. Place shrimp on skewers. Grill for 15 minutes, basting with remaining barbecue sauce. Serve with melted butter. Serves 4

GOVERNOR WALTER J. HICKEL FISH FILLETS IN SOUR CREAM SAUCE
A FAVORITE AT THE GOVERNOR'S HOUSE IN JUNEAU, ALASKA

INGREDIENTS:
1	lb. fish fillets, halibut is good
1	cup of sour cream
2	tablespoons of minced onion
1	tablespoon of chopped parsley
1/4	teaspoon of dry mustard
2	tablespoons of chopped dill pickle
2	tablespoons of chopped green pepper (opt.)
1	tablespoon of lemon juice
1/4	teaspoon of sweet basil
1/4	teaspoon of paprika
	salt and pepper to taste

DIRECTIONS:
Arrange fish in buttered baking dish. Salt and pepper to taste. Combine remaining ingredients and spread on fish. Sprinkle with paprika and bake 20-30 minutes in a 375 degree oven.

Food Proverb
Variety is the SPICE of life.
What do you think this
means _____

_____

Seafood 130

SENATOR LAUCH FAIRCLOTH OYSTER CASSEROLE

INGREDIENTS:

24-28	standard oysters, shelled
3-1/2	tablespoons of butter (plus extra)
1-1/2	cups of water
1	chicken bouillon cube
3	tablespoons of flour
2-1/2	cups of hot milk
	saltines, crumbled
	butter

DIRECTIONS:

Preheat oven to 350 degrees. Place oysters in saucepan, with 1-1/2 tablespoons of butter, water and bouillon cube. Bring to boil and simmer for 8 minutes.

In a separate saucepan melt 2 tablespoons of butter and add flour. Stir to make roux. Slowly add 1/2 cup of hot milk to make a white sauce and set aside.

Drain oysters, reserving liquid. Add this liquid to 2 cups hot milk and bring to boil. Add the white sauce and whip until smooth and simmer until sauce is medium thick. (If sauce does not thicken as well as you would like, mix a little sauce with 2 to 3 teaspoons of flour in a cup and add back to sauce).

Spread a little sauce in the bottom of the casserole dish. Sprinkle with cracker crumbs mixed with a little butter. (you do not want soggy cracker crumbs, just a little taste of butter). Place oysters on cracker crumbs and cover with remaining sauce. Sprinkle buttered cracker crumbs over sauce. Bake for 30 minutes. ENJOY!

Serves 4.

Soup

SOUP
MISSOURI APPLE SOUP, PAGE 138
BEAN SOUP, PAGE 135
GAZPACHO SOUP, PAGE 133
LENTIL SOUP, PAGE 134
INSTANT MEATBALL SOUP, PAGE 137
SANTE FE SOUP, PAGE 136

SENATOR HOWARD M. METZENBAUM GAZPACHO SOUP

THIS IS A FAVORITE RECIPE OF MINE THAT IS BOTH "HEART SMART" AND FUN.

INGREDIENTS: *Howard M. Metzenbaum*

- 3 cans of tomato juice
- 1 cucumber - cut up fairly fine
- 1 green pepper - cut up fairly fine
- 1 clove of garlic - mashed
- 2 tablespoons of olive oil
- 1 tablespoon white wine vinegar
- 1/4 teaspoon tabasco sauce
- 1/2 cup of ice water

DIRECTIONS:
Blend all of the above ingredients and keep in the refrigerator. Tastes better if made a day ahead. Serve with toppings of croutons, chopped eggs, etc. Season to taste.
Serves 4.

SENATOR ALFONSE D'AMATO LENTIL SOUP

INGREDIENTS: *Alfonse D'Amato*

4	slices bacon, cut in small pieces
1	clove garlic
3	tablespoons tomato sauce
2	cups water
1	cup of lentils
1	tablespoon chopped fresh parsley

DIRECTIONS:
Wash lentils under cold water. Drain. Saute bacon in large saucepan with garlic clove until clove is golden brown. Remove garlic. Stir in tomato sauce. Add water. Let soup base cook until rolling boil.
Add lentils to base.
Let cook over medium heat, adding more water as needed during cooking. When lentils are tender in 30 to 45 minutes, add fresh parsley, salt and pepper to taste.
Yield: 3 servings.

NOTE: Small boiled pasta (macaroni) may be added to soup before serving.

Food Proverb
Too many cooks spoil the soup
What do you think this means _____

The Famous Senate Restaurant BEAN SOUP RECIPE, was submitted by Senator CARL LEVIN

HISTORY OF SENATE BEAN SOUP

Carl Levin

Whatever uncertainties may exist in the Senate of the United States, one thing is sure: Bean Soup is on the menu of the Senate Restaurant every day.

The origin of this culinary decree has been lost in antiquity, but there are several oft-repeated legends.

One story has it that Senator Fred Thomas Dubois of Idaho, who served in the Senate from 1901 to 1907, when Chairman of the Committee that supervised the Senate Restaurant, gaveled through a resolution requiring that bean soup be on the menu every day.

Another account attributes the bean soup mandate to Senator Knute Nelson of Minnesota, who expressed his fondness for it in 1903.

In any case, Senators and their guests are always assured of a hearty, nourishing dish; they know they can rely upon it's delightful flavor and epicurean qualities.

The Famous Senate Restaurant
Bean Soup Recipe

*Take two pounds of small **Michigan Navy Beans**, wash, and run through hot water until the Beans are white again. Put on the fire with four quarts of hot water. Then take one and one-half pounds of Smoked Ham Hocks, boil slowly approximately three hours in a covered pot. Braise one onion chopped in a little butter, and, when light brown, put in the Bean Soup. Season with salt and pepper, then serve. Do not add salt until ready to serves. (Serves eight persons).*

AMANDA GREGORY 1994 A-OK COOK-OFF JUNIOR CHAMPION STATE OF OKLAHOMA SANTE FE SOUP

SANTA FE SOUP

INGREDIENTS:
- 1 pound of lean ground beef
- 2 cans (16 ounces) Best Yet pinto beans
- 1 can (15-1/4 ounces) Best Yet kidney beans
- 1 can (14-1/2 ounces) Best Yet stewed tomatoes undrained and chopped
- 1 package (1.25 ounces) Cedar Hill taco seasoning mix
- 1 can (10 ounces) Rotel tomatoes, undrained
- 1 envelope (1 ounce) ranch dressing mix
- 1 can (16 ounces) Best Yet whole kernel corn
- 1/4 cup of onion, chopped
- 1/2 cup of water
- 1/4 teaspoon of salt, if desired

DIRECTIONS:
In a large skillet brown ground beef over medium heat; drain. In Dutch oven combine ground beef and remaining ingredients. Bring to a boil. Reduce heat, cover and simmer 15 minutes.
Yield: 6 to 8 servings

SENATOR ALFONSE D'AMATO INSTANT MEATBALL SOUP

Alfonse D'Amato

Fighting inflation at the supermarket may be the toughest battle of all for "THE FORGOTTEN MIDDLE CLASS." Most of the federal regulations that stifle business and private enterprise are passed along to us - the consumer - in the form of higher prices at the check-out counter. Over the years, I have discovered that many of my family's favorite dishes are not only easy to prepare but also economical. More importantly, they are flavorful and nutritious.

Enjoy these "recipes for the forgotten middle class." By sharing this collection of our favorites with you, I hope they will help ease the pinch on your family's food budget.

INSTANT MEATBALL SOUP

- 2 large carrots, peeled and cubed
- 3 large celery stalks, diced
- 1 medium-sized onion, diced
- 4 cups of water
- 4 chicken bouillon cubes
- 1/2 lb. ground beef
- 1/2 cup of grated cheese, romano or parmesan

Boil water in large saucepan or soup kettle. Add carrots, celery and onion. Cover and let cook until vegetables are tender. Add bouillon cubes and simmer.

Season ground beef with salt and pepper and shape beef into tiny meatballs 1/2 inch in size.

Add meatballs to soup, cooking from 3 to 5 minutes.

Serve with grated cheese.

Yield: 2 to 3 servings

NOTE: Boiled pasta or rice may be added before serving.

SENATOR CHRISTOPHER "KIT" BOND MISSOURI APPLE SOUP

Christopher S. Bond

MISSOURI APPLE SOUP

- 2 tablespoons of butter
- 2 medium onions, thinly sliced
- 6 red Jonathan apples, peeled, cored and diced
- 4 cups of chicken broth
- 2 tablespoons of sugar
- 1 tablespoon of curry powder, or to taste
-   salt and freshly ground white pepper to taste
- 1-2 cups light cream (to taste)

In a Dutch oven, melt butter, saute onions until transparent. Add apples, broth, sugar and curry powder. Season with salt and pepper. Cook covered over low heat until apples are soft.

Strain apples and onions from the broth and reserve, set broth aside. Place apples and onions in a food processor or blender and puree. Add broth, blend well. Add cream according to desired richness, chill. Taste and adjust seasoning. Garnish with thin apple wedges and a sprinkling of sliced almonds.

10 to 12 servings.

Vegetables

BROCCOLI CHEESE QUICHE, PAGE 140
CARROT CASSEROLE 1981, PAGE 142
POTATO CASSEROLE, PAGE 141
POTATO SILVER STATE, PAGE 142
FRENCH-CUT STRING BEANS, PAGE 139

SENATOR ALFONSE D'AMATO FRENCH-CUT STRING BEANS

INGREDIENTS:

1	lb. fresh string beans
1/4	cup of corn oil
5	tablespoons of tomato sauce
1/4	cup of grated cheese, romano or parmesan
1	clove garlic, finely chopped
1	teaspoon of oregano
1/4	cup of water

DIRECTIONS:
Wash string beans and drain. Cut beans french-style (cut lengthwise). Placed sliced beans in heavy skillet, adding water, oil, tomato sauce, oregano, garlic and grated cheese. Salt and pepper to taste. Cover skillet tightly. Cook over low-medium heat for about 20 minutes or until beans are slightly firm but tender.
Yield: 4 servings

GOVERNOR TOMMY G. THOMPSON BROCCOLI CHEESE QUICHE

BROCCOLI CHEESE QUICHE

INGREDIENTS:
- 1-1/2 cups of chopped broccoli
- 1-1/2 cups of grated cheddar cheese
- 4 eggs
- 1-1/2 cups of cream
- 1/4 teaspoon salt
- 1 pastry for 10 inch pie crust
- dash pepper
- dash nutmeg

DIRECTIONS:
Arrange broccoli and cheese in pastry-lined pan. Beat together eggs, cream and spices in bowl. Pour the custard like mixture over cheese and broccoli. Place in preheated oven at 375 degrees for 35-40 minutes or until top is golden brown and knife inserted one inch from the edge comes out clean.
Serving: 8 main dish servings.

Food Proverb
Don't bite off more than you can chew.
What do you think this means _____

Vegetables 140

GOVERNOR E. BENJAMIN NELSON POTATO CASSEROLE

POTATO CASSEROLE
INGREDIENTS:
- 2 lbs. frozen hash brown potatoes
- 1/2 cup of melted butter
- 1 teaspoon of salt
- 1/4 teaspoon of pepper
- 1/2 cup of onion, chopped
- 1/2 cup of cream of potato soup or cream of chicken soup
- 1 pt. sour cream with chives
- 2 cups of grated cheddar cheese
- 1/2 cup of celery, chopped

DIRECTIONS:
Defrost potatoes. Combine melted butter, salt, pepper, soup and sour cream. Mix hash browns with onion, celery and cheese. Mix in soup mixture. Pour into a greased 9x12 inch casserole dish.
Serves 16

TOPPING:
- 2 cups crushed potato chips
- 1/2 cup of melted butter

Mix butter and chips. Sprinkle on top of casserole. Bake 45 minutes at 350 degrees. This dish can be frozen and reheated before serving.

GOVERNOR BOB MILLER SILVER STATE POTATOES

4	medium potatoes, boiled, peeled and grated
2	cups of sour cream
1	tablespoon of salt
1/4	cup of milk
1/4	cup of butter
1	regular can of cream of chicken soup
1/2	cup of grated cheddar cheese
1/2	cup of chopped onion
	corn flakes

Combine all ingredients except potatoes. Simmer on low heat until cheese melts. Add potatoes. Place into lightly greased baking dish. Top with crushed corn flakes mixed with softened butter. Bake at 350 degrees approximately one hour or until golden brown. Freezes and reheats well.

GRACE and BILL SAYRE CARROT CASSEROLE 1981

3	cups of her stuffing mix plus rice
2	tablespoons of butter
1/4	cup onion, chopped
1	10 ounce can celery soup
3/4	cup shredded cheddar cheese
	salt and pepper to taste
5	cups sliced cooked carrots
1/3	cup of melted butter

Prepare stuffing as directed, set aside. Melt 3 tablespoons of butter, add onion, saute. Add soup and cheese stirring until heated and cheese melted. Season, add carrots and turn into greased 2 quart casserole dish. Cover carrots with stuffing. Drizzle 1/3 cup melted butter on top and bake in 350 degree oven for 20 minutes.

THE ORGANIZER

We all know the frustration of trying to find a certain recipe we saw in another cookbook or magazine. The recipe that sounded so good, we clipped and stashed it for safe-keeping only to find that, we hid it too well. The Recipe Organizer allows you to keep all your favorite recipes together in one place. Simply enter recipes on the ready to be filled in pages, or insert the data (as to where it can be found) into the Organizer Index space, at the bottom of each page, and enter it later, when your schedule permits.

Get Organized!

CENTRALIZE YOUR RECIPES. This eliminates searching every Cookbook, back dated magazines, used envelopes, mayonnaise jars, scraps of paper, or 3x5 index cards or the entire cookbook section of the Library looking for that wonderful but misplaced, never to be found again recipe.

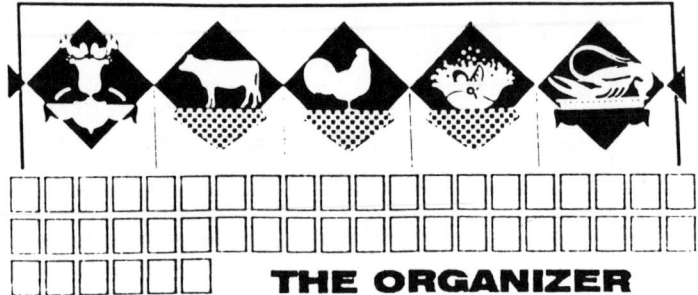

THE ORGANIZER

Name of Recipe _____

Ingredients:

_____ _____
_____ _____
_____ _____
_____ _____
_____ _____

Directions _____
_____
_____
_____
_____
_____
_____
_____
_____
_____
_____
_____
_____

Serves _____

THE ORGANIZER INDEX ... Enter the recipe later from this information. Look in :

Book _____ **page** _____
Magazine _____ **page** _____
Other _____ **page** _____

MY FAVORITE RECIPE

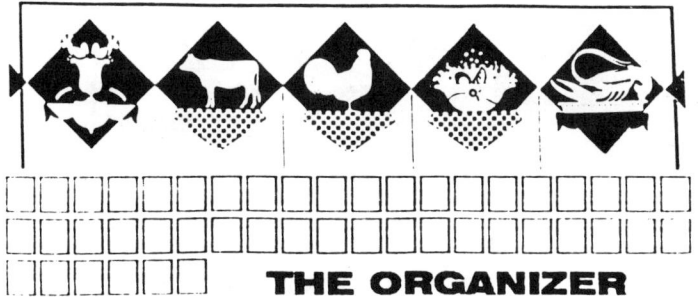

THE ORGANIZER

Name of Recipe_____

Ingredients:

_____ _____
_____ _____
_____ _____
_____ _____
_____ _____

Directions_____
_____
_____
_____
_____
_____
_____
_____
_____
_____
_____
_____
_____

Serves_____

THE ORGANIZER INDEX ... Enter the recipe later from this information. Look in :

Book _____page_____
Magazine _____page_____
Other _____page_____

MY FAVORITE RECIPE

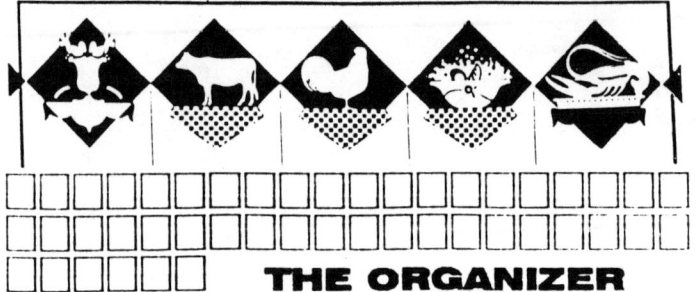

THE ORGANIZER

Name of Recipe_____

Ingredients:
_____ _____
_____ _____
_____ _____
_____ _____
_____ _____

Directions_____
_____
_____
_____
_____
_____
_____
_____
_____
_____
_____
_____

Serves_____

THE ORGANIZER INDEX ... Enter the recipe later from this information. Look in :

Book _____page_____
Magazine _____page_____
Other _____page_____

MY FAVORITE RECIPE

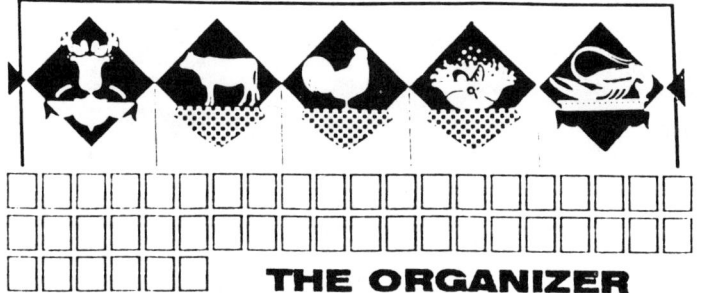

THE ORGANIZER

Name of Recipe _____

Ingredients:

_____ _____
_____ _____
_____ _____
_____ _____
_____ _____

Directions _____
_____
_____
_____
_____
_____
_____
_____
____ _____
____ _____
_____
_____
_____

Serves _____

THE ORGANIZER INDEX ... Enter the recipe later from this information. Look in :

Book _____ page _____
Magazine _____ page _____
Other _____ page _____

MY FAVORITE RECIPE

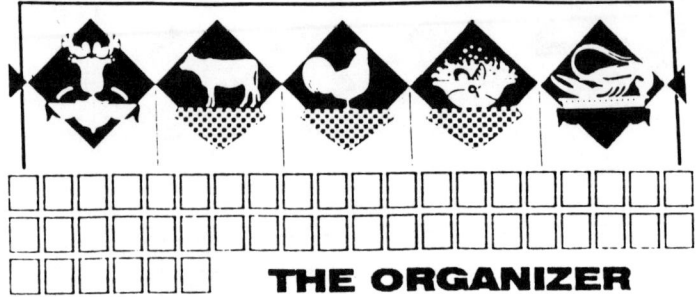

THE ORGANIZER

Name of Recipe _____

Ingredients:
_____ _____
_____ _____
_____ _____
_____ _____
_____ _____

Directions _____
_____
_____
_____
_____
_____
_____
_____
_____
_____
_____
_____

Serves _____

THE ORGANIZER INDEX ... Enter the recipe later from this information. Look in :

Book _____ page _____
Magazine _____ page _____
Other _____ page _____

MY FAVORITE RECIPE

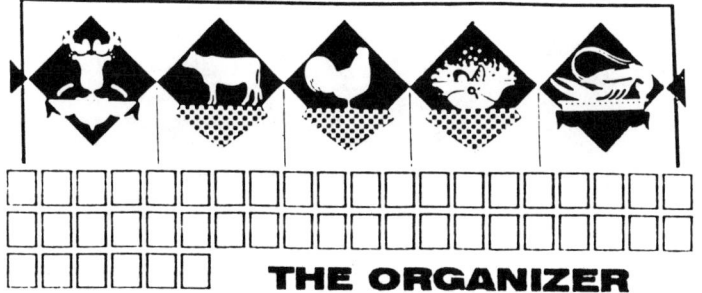

THE ORGANIZER

Name of Recipe_____

Ingredients:

_____   _____
_____   _____
_____   _____
_____   _____
_____

Directions_____
_____
_____
_____
_____
_____
_____
_____
_____
_____
_____
_____
_____

Serves_____

THE ORGANIZER INDEX ... Enter the recipe later from this information. Look in:

Book _____ page _____
Magazine _____ page _____
Other _____ page _____

MY FAVORITE RECIPE

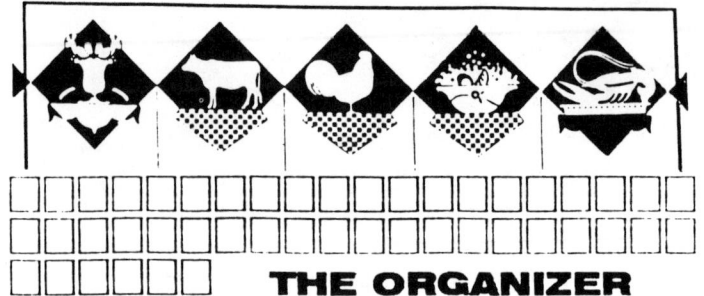

THE ORGANIZER

Name of Recipe _____

Ingredients:

_____   _____
_____   _____
_____   _____
_____   _____

Directions _____
_____
_____
_____
_____
_____
_____
_____
_____
_____
_____
_____
_____

Serves _____

THE ORGANIZER INDEX ... Enter the recipe later from this information. Look in :

Book _____ page _____
Magazine _____ page _____
Other _____ page _____

MY FAVORITE RECIPE

INDEX

A ----------------------------

Ambrosia, fruit and nut mold, 107
Anchovy, garlic bread, 22
Antipasto, Joe Paterno, 11
APPETIZERS (see page 9)
   Antipasto, 11
   Artichoke, Ernani, 10
   Pepper roasted rainbow, 12
APPLES
   Apple cake, fresh, 31
   Apple cake, Norwegian, 39
   Apple walnut, 106
   Pie, Granny's, 72
   Salad, 106
   Soup, Missouri, 138
Artichokes, Ernani, 10
Avocado, salsa, 118

B ----------------------------

Baked rice, 97
Baked shad & roe, 121
Barbecue chicken, 84
Barbecue shrimp, 129
BEANS
   Beans, baked, sausage, 64
   Beans and sausage, Carol's black, 58
   Bean soup, 135
   Lentil soup, 134
   French cut, 139
Beef broil, light & lean, 51
BEVERAGES (see page 9)
   Lemonade, 13
   Wassail, 9
Biscochitos, 47
Blender cheesecake, Ann Simpson's, 30
Blueberry buckle, 34
Brains'n eggs, pork, Southern delight, 104
Bran muffins, 20
Bran muffins, Mary's, 19

BREADS (see page 15)
   Corn bread, 16
   Cranberry Massachusetts, 17
   Garlic with anchovy, 22
   Honey, whole grain, 18
   Peach bread, Georgia, 15
Broccoli-cheese Quiche, 140
Broccoli-chicken, casseroles, 80
BROWNIES (see page 42)
   Chocolate double, brownies, 43
   Mint stick brownies, 42
Burgoo, 62

C ----------------------------

Cajun deep fried turkey, 76
Cajun sauce for dipping, 117
CAKES (See page 25)
   Apple cake, fresh, 31
   Apple cake, Norwegian, 39
   Blueberry buckle, 34
   Caramel pineapple, Joan Specter's, 32
   Carrot cake, 26
   Cheesecake, chocolate, 40
   Coconut cake, 25
   Maple syrup cake, 33
   Mississippi Mud cake, 41
   Molasses cake, Nanny's, 27
   Orange cake, Penn State University, 28
   Pecan cake, chocolate, 37
   Pudding, chocolate steamed, 29
   Yum yum, cake, 38
CASSEROLES
   Broccoli-chicken, 80
   Carrot 1981, casserole, 142
   Chicken enchilada, 86
   Oyster casserole, 131
   Potato casserole, 141
CHEESE
   Cheese pie, 70

Cheesy chicken enchiladas, 82
Broccoli-cheese, Quiche, 140
San Francisco, pie, 49
CHEESECAKES
　Ann Simpson's, 30
　Chocolate cheesecake, 40
Chews, Chinese, 48
CHICKEN (see page 75)
　Barbecue chicken, 84
　Broccoli-chicken, 80
　Cutlets Ala Russe, 78
　Enchilada casserole, 86
　Enchiladas, cheesy, 82
　Fajitas, 80
　Korean, 75
　Mrs. Coverdell's, 83
　Mrs. Tipper Gore's family favorite chicken, 77
　Oriental chicken, salad, 85
　Parmesan, 81
　Roll-up, Annie's Little, 88
　Scallopini, 79
Chili
　Con Carne, 56
　Gramm's award winning, 55
Chinese, chews, 48
Chip, dip, 117
CHOCOLATE
　Brownies, double, 43
　Cheesecake, 40
　Coconut cake, 25
　Fresh mint, 35
　Ice cream pie, 70
　Mint stick, 42
　Nugget, 36
　Pecan cake, 37
　Pudding, steamed, 29
　Schaefer's wafers, 73
COOKIES (see page 44)
　Biscochitos, 47
　Chews, Chinese, 48
　Grandmother Merrick's, 45
　Mint, French, 35

Nut bar, toffee, 46
Schaefer's wafers, 49
Sour-cream, sugar, 44
Corn bread, 16
CRABS
　Blue, steamed, 123
　Cakes, Norfolk, 128
　How to open steamed crabs, 123
　Supreme, crabmeat, 121
Cranberry bread, Massachusetts, 17
Crepes, 8 large Nalesz Niki, 96
Cutlets Ala Russe, 78

D———————————

DIPS (see page 115)
　Avocado salsa, 118
　Cajun, 117
　Chip, 117
　Garbanzo, 118
　Paprika, 116
　Shrimp, 115
　Sour cream, 116
Dove on the grill, 84

E———————————

Eggs, Kugel, Mr. L's, 98
Eggs and Pork brains, 104

F———————————

Fajitas, chicken, 80
FISH (see page 75)
　Fillets, sour cream, 130
　Halibut, parmesan, 122
　Halibut, sweet & sour, 125
　Katfish, South of the Border, 126
　Red snapper, 119
　Salmonburgers, 122
　Shad and Roe, baked, 121

Sole, fillet, 120
Food handling, safe, 68
French mint, 35
Fresh apple cake, 31
Fruit & nut mold, Ambrosia, 107

G——————————————

Garbanzo dip, 118
Garlic bread with anchovy, 22
Gazpacho soup, 133
Georgia peach bread, 15
Grandmother Merrick's cookies, 45
Granny's recipes, adapt, 14
Gumbo, seafood, 124

H——————————————

Halibut
  Parmesan, 122
  Sweet and sour, 125
Hero, Hard rock minners, 23
Holiday menus, 110-113
Honey, whole grain, bread, 18
How to adapt Granny's, recipes to healthier eating, 14
How to carve a turkey, 24
How to choose healthier foods, 91
How to cook a perfect turkey, 24
How to read the new food label, 102-103

I-L——————————————

Ice cream pie, 70
Instant meatball soup, 137
Italian sausage & beans, 64
Korean chicken, 75

Kugel, Mr. L's, 98
Lasagna, Ann & Fife's, 67
Lemon
  Mousse, 71
  Pie, Mary's best 69
Lemonade, 9
Lentil soup, 134
Lite & lean, beef broil, 51

M——————————————

Maple syrup cake, 33
Massachusetts, cranberry, 17
MEAT (see page 51)
Beans
  Baked bean & Italian sausage, 64
  Beans and sausage, Carol's black bean, 58
Beef broil, lite and lean, 51
Burgoo, 62
Chili
  Con carne, 56
  Gramm's award winning, 55
Meatballs
  Meatballs, 54
  Meatball soup, instant, 137
  Montana easy Taco, meatballs, 61
Pork
  Brains'n eggs, Southern delight, 104
  chops, broiled, 60
  chops, pepper, 57
  Sausage & black bean, 58
  Sausage souffle, 54
  Spareribs, sweet & sour, 53
Taco
  Taco meatballs, Montana easy, 61
  Taco salad, South Dakota, 59
Mint, French, 35
Mint, stick brownies, 42
Mississippi mud cake, 41
Molasses cake, Nanny's, 27

Molasses cookies,
   Grandmother Merrick's, 45
MUFFINS (see page 19)
Bran
  Bran muffins, 20
  Bran muffins, Mary's, 19
  Oat bran muffins, 21

N————————————

Nanny's molasses, cake, 27
Nalesz Niki, 96
Norfolk crab cakes, 128
Norwegian apple cake, 39
Nugget, chocolate, 36
Nut bar, toffee, 46

O————————————

Oat, bran muffins, 21
Orange cake, Penn State
     University, 28
Organizer pages, 143
Oyster casserole, 131

P————————————

Pancakes, Nalez Niki, 96
Paprika sauce, 116
Parenting recipe, 109
PASTA (see page 65)
Lasagna, Ann & Fife's, 67
Spaghetti
  Clam sauce, 66
  Garlic & oil, 65
Pepper Pork chops, 57
Pepper, roasted, rainbow, 12
PIES (see page 69)
  Apple pie, Granny's, 72
Cheese
  Cheese pie, 70
  San Francisco, 49
Ice cream, pie, 70
Lemon
  lemon mousse, 71
  lemon pie, Mary's best, 69

Peach pie, creamy, 74
Pecan pie, Georgia, 71
Peach bread, Georgia, 15
Penn State orange cake, 28
Pineapple caramel, Joan
     Specter's, 32
Pita pockets, grilled, 87
Pork brains'n eggs,
    Southern Delight, 104
Potatoes
  Casserole, 141
  Salad, 106
  Silver State, 142
POULTRY (see page 75)
Chicken
  Barbecue chicken, 84
  Broccoli chicken,
     casserole, 80
  Burgoo, 62
  Cutlet Ala Russe, 78
  Enchilada, casserole, 86
  Enchilada, cheesy, 82
  Fajitas, 80
  Korean, 75
  Mrs. Coverdell's, 83
  Mrs. Tipper Gore's family
    favorite, 77
  Parmesan, 81
  Roll-up, Annie's Little, 88
  Salad, Oriental, 85
  Scallopini, 79
Pudding, chocolate, 29
Turkey
  Sopa, 89
  Cajun deep fried, 76
  Grilled Pita pockets, 87

Q————————————

Quiche
  Broccoli-cheese, 140
  Lorraine, 100

R————————————

RICE (see page 95)
  Baked, 97
  Dressing, Grandma
        Daigle's, 99
  Hoppin' John, 101
  Pilaf, pistachio, 95

S----------

Safe food handling, 68
SALAD (see page 105)
  Apple salad, 106
  Fruit & nut mold,
        Ambrosia, 107
  Oriental chicken salad, 85
  Potato salad, 106
  Spinach salad, 108
  Taco salad,
    South Dakota, 59
  Tomato & onion salad, 108
Salmonburgers, 122
Sandwich, Hardrock Hero, 23
San Francisco cheese pie, 49
Santa Fe soup, 136
SAUCE (see page 116)
  Avocado, 118
  Cajun for dipping, 117
  Paprika sauce, 116
  Sour cream sauce, 116
Sausage
  Sausage & baked beans, 64
  Sausage & black bean, 58
  Sausage souffle, 54
SEAFOOD (see page 119)
  Crab cakes, Norfolk, 128
  Crabmeat supreme, 121
  Crabs, blue steamed, 123
  Fish fillets, sour cream, 130
  Halibut parmesan, 122
  Halibut, sweet & sour, 125
  Katfish South of the
    border, 126
  Oyster casserole, 131
  Red snapper, 119
  Salmonburgers, 122

  Seafood Gumbo, 124
  Shad & Roe, baked, 121
  Shrimp bowl, recipe, 127
  Shrimp, barbecue, 129
  Sole, fillet, 120
Schaefer's Wafers, 73
Shrimp dip, 115
SOUP (see page 133)
  Apple soup, Missouri
  Bean soup, Senate, 135
  Gazpacho soup, 133
  Instant meatball soup, 137
  Lentil soup, 134
  Santa Fe soup, 136
Southern delight, pork
    brains'n eggs, 104
Spaghetti
  Clams, 66
  Garlic & oil, 65
Spareribs, sweet & sour, 53
Spinach salad, 108
Steamed crabs, 123

T----------

Taco
  Taco meatballs, Montana.
    easy, 61
  Taco salad,
    South Dakota, 59
Terms, cooking & Rest., 50
Toffee nut bar, 46
Tomato beef, 52
Tomato & onion, 108
TURKEY (see page 75)
  Cajun deep fried, 76
  Grilled Pita pockets, 87
  Turkey sopa, 89
Turkey, how to carve, 24

U-V----------

VEGETABLES (page, 139)
  Broccoli-cheese quiche, 140
  Carrot casserole, 1981, 142

Potato casserole, 141
Potato, Silver State, 142
String beans,
    French-cut, 139
Vegetable salad, 105

W———————————

Wafers, Schaefer's, 73
Wassail, 9
We the People invite, 63

X-Y-Z———————————

Yum Yum cake, 38

BOOKMARKS

I hope you enjoy this cookbook and the many meals that are produced from its pages. I think that you will find this cookbook, whether it's for you, or a gift for that special person, to be a perfect addition to any kitchen.

TO ORDER:

Please send me_____copies of the Famous People Cookbook...What's Cookin' in the U.S.A. Each book is $12.95 (payable in U.S. funds). Make check or money order payable to:
BRIGHT IDEAS IN MARKETING PUBLICATIONS
P.O. BOX 494
BROOMALL, PA. 19008
(please print)
NAME_____

ADDRESS_____

CITY_____

STATE_____ZIP_____

Allow 6 to 8 weeks for delivery. Prices are subject to change without notice. Postage and handling: $ 3.00 for one book, add .50 cents to each additional book.

Total Books ordered_____ x $12.95 = ____		
Shipping & Handling $ 3.00 _____ (add .50 cents to each additional book ordered)	$3	00
Total Books ordered x .50 = _____		
Applicable Sales Tax_____		
Total amount enclosed_____		

TO ORDER:

Please send me_____copies of the Famous People Cookbook...What's Cookin' in the U.S.A. Each book is $12.95 (payable in U.S. funds). Make check or money order payable to:
BRIGHT IDEAS IN MARKETING PUBLICATIONS
P.O. BOX 494
BROOMALL, PA. 19008
(please print)
NAME_____

ADDRESS_____

CITY_____

STATE_____ZIP_____

Allow 6 to 8 weeks for delivery. Prices are subject to change without notice. Postage and handling: $ 3.00 for one book, add .50 cents to each additional book.

Total Books ordered_____ x $12.95 = ____		
Shipping & Handling $ 3.00 _____ (add .50 cents to each additional book ordered)	$3	00
Total Books ordered x .50 = _____		
Applicable Sales Tax_____		
Total amount enclosed_____		

Thanks	Thanks
Thanks	Thanks
Thanks	Thanks
Thanks	Thanks
Thanks	Thanks
Thanks	Thanks
Thanks	Thanks
Thanks	Thanks